LOST LINES
East Anglia
Nigel Welbourn

Ian Allan
PUBLISHING

This book is dedicated to Mary Welbourn,
the author's mother, who died in 2013.

Abbreviations

BR — British Railways
CVH — Colne Valley & Halstead Railway
GER — Great Eastern Railway
GN&GE — Great Northern & Great Eastern Joint Committee
LNER — London & North Eastern Railway
M&GN — Midland & Great Northern Joint Railway
MR — Midland Railway
MSL — Mid-Suffolk Light Railway
NSJ — Norfolk & Suffolk Joint Railway

Key to maps:

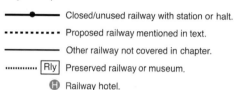

━━━●━━━ Closed/unused railway with station or halt.
▪▪▪▪▪▪▪▪▪▪▪ Proposed railway mentioned in text.
━━━━━━━ Other railway not covered in chapter.
▪▪▪▪▪▪▪▪ Rly Preserved railway or museum.
Ⓗ Railway hotel.

First published 2014

ISBN 978 0 7110 3748 9

© Nigel Welbourn 2014

Published by Ian Allan Publishing Ltd, Hersham,
Surrey KT12 4RG.

Printed in England.

Visit the Ian Allan Publishing website at
www.ianallanpublishing.com

Picture credits
Every effort has been made to identify and correctly attribute photographic credits. Should any error have occurred this is entirely unintentional.

Contents

Front cover, top: 'B17/6' No 61656 leaves St Olaves station September 1958. *Courtesy Colour-Rail*

Front cover, bottom: 'J15' No 65475 rolling into Lavenham July 1959. *Courtesy Colour-Rail*

Back cover: A Cravens DMU waits at Brightlingsea shortly before closure in 1963. *Courtesy Colour-Rail*

Title page: A Class 'J15' waits while the level crossing gates are opened by the engine crew, near Brockford on the ex-MSL, on 14 June 1952. Although a rural idyll, the train was in reality travelling slowly to fields in the middle of nowhere. Such lines were early candidates for closure, with services ending on this route the following month. *R. E. Vincent*

Facing page: Ex-GER Class 'E4' 2-4-0 No 62785 seen at Mildenhall in 1959. Built in 1894 this was the last 2-4-0 engine to remain in work in Britain and was subsequently preserved. *Courtesy Colour-Rail*

Introduction

The lost lines of East Anglia are as distinctive as the area itself. They were particularly dependent on agricultural freight, which for generations had been the main activity in the region. They served many remote rural backwaters that were unlikely ever to provide revenues matching those of railways in the industrialised regions of the country. Even the industries served were largely connected with agriculture, and the GER was sometimes called 'The swede'.

There was also heavy summer tourism to and from the East Coast resorts. At its zenith every town of any size in East Anglia was served by the railway network. The GER was particularly dominant in the area, but a number of other railways were also to be found, in particular the long tentacles of the M&GN.

Some rationalisations were made when the LNER took over in 1923, but the overall network remained largely intact. Nationalisation in 1948 saw the creation of the Eastern Region of BR. A growing number of branches lost their passenger services, but at first the majority of lines survived. Nonetheless rail traffic was increasingly being lost to the roads. With mounting losses, almost the entire ex-M&GN network was closed in 1959 – a bitter foretaste of what was to follow.

The infamous Beeching Report of 1963 was to recommend wholesale closures. Recognising that irrevocable change was on the way, the railways of East Anglia have been recorded by your author for more than 50 years. This book examines the decline culminating in closure, which has left huge rural areas of East Anglia without any railway services, but equally providing a fascinating legacy of lost railway remains.

More than 30 closed railways in East Anglia are covered, including some lines explicitly linked to the region. Such was the scale of closures in East Anglia that this book does not duplicate any of the images or content of the companion volume *Lost Lines: Eastern*, so that the two books are both freestanding and complement each other.

Beeching and beyond

The *Reshaping of British Railways* report was published in March 1963 and was widely known as the Beeching Report, Dr Richard Beeching being Chairman of BR at the time. Its main recommendations proposed the mass closure of much of the railway network in Britain, in an effort to secure profitability.

The Beeching Report was unpopular, and when he was kicked by a railway employee I was delighted. The passage of time has not mellowed my view and I am going to give him my own kicking now. In my opinion he was an individual whose patronising style disguised a lack of real understanding of his new responsibilities in the railway industry.

The Report ignored wider economic and social issues and did not properly address matters of fares and pricing, while calculations of the losses for some secondary lines were distorted to increase costs. Furthermore the contribution made by secondary routes to the wider network, together with the effect of economies on such lines, as an alternative to the easy option of closure, was not considered. The principle of closing duplicated routes was taken to absurd extremes and no attempt was made to protect routes for possible long-term future reopening.

The Report's traffic survey was flawed; for example, the revenue collected at coastal destinations would always be minimal. A more accurate survey would be that used by the LNER, based on the number of tickets collected at such destinations. The timing of the survey, for just one week in April, ensured that the detailed list of closures was also flawed.

The result of Dr Beeching and his Report? The railway network was fatally reduced and went on to lose even more money – his plan was a failure. In his defence, government transport ministers made the actual decisions to close routes. In East Anglia even Dr Beeching did not recommend the closure of Wisbech, Swaffham, Hunstanton or the Cambridge-Oxford line, and of course it is easy to criticise with hindsight.

Facing page The final day of services on the ex-MSL: gleaming in the morning sunshine, wreath-decorated, Class 'J15' 0-6-0 No 65447 climbs away from Haughley with the 11.15am train to Laxfield. The usual number of passenger coaches had been doubled for the closing runs. The view here, on 26 July 1952, predates the Beeching closures by a decade. G. Mortimer

Below The Sheringham-Melton Constable section of the ex-M&GN soon became prey to Dr Beeching, closing to all remaining traffic in December 1964. After a period of dereliction, by the date of this September 1971 photograph the roof of the Melton Constable platform buildings had been stripped of slates and soon the entire station building would be demolished. T. Hepburn

As a consequence of the Report, in August of that year a schoolboy walked to Woodbridge station, went into the booking office and purchased a ticket to Aldeburgh – simply because all the stations were threatened with closure in the report. The signals at Woodbridge were pulled to 'clear' and a relatively new two-coach DMU pulled into the station. The train was not well patronised and a front seat behind the driver was soon occupied. The sound of an electric buzzer, the hiss of the air brakes, a hoot of the horn and, with a wave from the crossing-keeper, the train set off.

The schoolboy was your author and for me it was the start of a love affair with railways that were threatened with closure that has lasted to this day. I intended to visit every line proposed for closure in the Report. I was just 14 at the time and, with limited funds, my objective was not met, but I did visit every line that was proposed for closure in East Anglia.

So what was different half a century ago? Taking Woodbridge and Aldeburgh as examples, both had goods yards, and coal still arrived by rail at many local stations. But even then change was on the way; the goods yard at Aldeburgh had closed in 1959, and Woodbridge would follow in 1966.

Above This is the Stour Valley line at Clare after closure, looking towards the castle bailey in the summer of 1969. The track remained rusting and increasingly overgrown until it was lifted in 1970 by A. King & Sons of Norwich. Clare station buildings are now part of a country park. *Ian Allan Library*

Facing page A map of the BR network in East Anglia in 1948. BR

At Aldeburgh, in 1963, the gas lamps were considered outdated, even more so the oil lamps of Thorpeness Halt with its old carriages as facilities. At Aldeburgh the signalling had been abandoned, but the box and signal posts and rusting sidings remained, the whole atmosphere being one of terminal decline.

Woodbridge still had a station master at this time and a porter; the latter cycled to work with his railway waistcoat. There were booking office staff and there was one GER ticket remaining in stock, a 1st Class single to London; 'Get your Dad to buy it,' they said. He never went on that single journey.

The railcars had stubs on the seat backs to put out cigarettes, while 'old' steam-heated carriages were hauled by new diesel locomotives. The one through train to and from London had a buffet, and the attendant, dressed in white, would walk through the train advising those on board of his products, as there were no electronic on-train announcements. My diary recounts that when the assassination of President Kennedy occurred in 1963 American airmen travelling to Woodbridge air base were drunk in the buffet, displaying the long links between the railways and airfields in East Anglia.

The staff were extremely friendly, to me at least. I could visit almost any signal box as a schoolboy and would be made welcome; they were just not busy. The spare time allowed them to make the interiors immaculate: polished signal lever handles, unblemished cream linoleum and coal stoves added to the atmosphere. The station staff often directed me towards railwayana and freely gave me their time and views. Rides on the footplate were also given, particularly at off-peak times. This of course was all before common sense was replaced by 'health and safety'.

The railway landscape of East Anglia has changed in many ways over 50 years; the neatly groomed cuttings and embankments, with vegetation burned and cut away from the edge of bridges, at first became unkempt, then covered with ever-growing foliage.

Lineside trees have obscured several views, but equally provide havens for wildlife. Farming practices have also changed the landscape; the burning of stubble left many a dead tree and hedgerow, fields have become larger, the onset of Dutch elm disease also changed the landscape in some areas, but the Scots pine trees planted at several GER locations still survive. In terms of wildlife seen from the train, the biggest change seems to be the 'March hares', once a joy to see with their dancing antics; their number seems far less today. Sadly, pheasants still end up splattered on the front of trains.

Many of the railways were coming to an end in the 1960s and much of the infrastructure was

Right Even after the track and other items of scrap value were taken, unwanted railway remains were to be observed throughout East Anglia. Here the remains of Bartlow signal box are seen, looking towards Haverhill in January 1979; it had last been used in 1967. *A. Muckley*

Below This is Bartlow signal box in August 2011, with the sapling trees seen earlier having taken over. In 2013 some remains were still to be found. This box replaced two signal boxes at Bartlow, which were merged into one as an economy measure by the LNER. *Copyright John Sutton Creative Commons Licence*

outdated and worn-out. After the last train ran, key items of scrap value were taken, often in a crude and untidy way, by scrap merchants, but lesser bits and pieces often remained. I rescued considerable small items of railwayana from derelict booking offices, lamp rooms and goods yards.

Much of the Beeching Report was implemented, leaving many melancholy disused stations littering the region in the 1960s, including Aldeburgh, but the

East Suffolk line and therefore Woodbridge survived. Gradually the usefulness and wider economic benefit of railways became recognised. Most closures ceased after the oil crisis of 1974. The railways went on to be privatised, the roads became congested and rail passenger numbers increased.

Today when I walk to Woodbridge station there is a café, a B&B in the station house and the taxi office is still in use. The trains in 2013 were slower on the East Suffolk line than they were 50 years before, but trains are busy again and sensible economies, together with investment in automatic level crossings, new signalling and passenger information systems, have been made. I can only wonder if Beeching had taken a more positive and flexible approach, whether the same would be the case elsewhere on several other lines now long closed.

Below The closure of lines in Norfolk under the Beeching plan left huge areas without rail transport. Wells-next-the-Sea, for example, was almost 20 miles by road from the nearest main-line station. The exterior of the terminus, dating from 1857, is seen here in June 2012, largely unchanged since its closure in 1964 and in use as a second-hand bookshop. *Author*

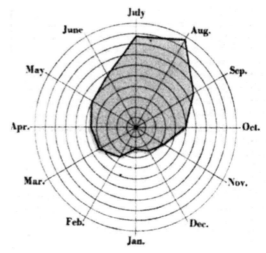

The graph shows number of tickets collected during each month of the year.

Each concentric ring represents 10,000 tickets.

Above LNER statistics for Suffolk in 1939. Note the massive disparity of ticket collections between April and August, one of several issues not properly factored into the Beeching Report. *Author's collection*

Sheringham......																			
Weybourne ..																			
Holt...........																			
Melton Constable																			

★ The train service between Sheringham and Melton Constable is withdrawn and Weybourne, Holt and Melton Constable stations are closed.

The locality is served by omnibuses operated by the Eastern Counties Omnibus Co. Ltd.

∗ The service between **North Walsham** and **Mundesley-on-Sea** may be withdrawn and **Paston and Knapton** and **Mundesley-on-Sea** stations may be closed during the currency of this time table and in this event appropriate notice will be given

Above Timetable closure information for Melton Constable and the impending closure of Mundesley-on-Sea, from the BR summer timetable, 1964.

Right Even where stations remained open it seemed as if every effort was made to make them unattractive. Here at Corton-on-Sea the ex-NSJ station building was allowed to become derelict even before closure. The remaining buildings are seen in the winter of 1970. *Author*

Facing page Superheated Class 'J17' 0-6-0 No 65551 is seen on 14 April 1951 at South Lynn, on the former M&GN. The station closed to passengers in February 1959, as part of the closure of almost all the M&GN network from the East Midlands to the Norfolk coast. South Lynn survived as a coal depot until May 1966 and a rusting line to the nearby sugar beet factory was extant until 1995. *R. Dean*

Above The closures and rationalisation of services resulted in about 16,000 carriages being scrapped under the Beeching proposals. The interior of a carriage heading for scrap is seen here on the Forncett-Wymondham branch in September 1964. The compartment had been heavily vandalised and many of the carriage prints would not survive the fiery destruction to follow. *Author*

Right The trackbed south of the former Lowestoft North station has been turned into 'The Great Eastern Linear Park', and is seen here in March 2012. The substantial bridge, one of almost 50 on the Lowestoft-Yarmouth route, together with its spacious loading gauge, reflects the late construction of the NSJ, which opened in 1903. The attractive use of a short section of trackbed is small consolation for the loss of the rail service. *Author*

2

Lost links to Anglia

Before the railways arrived, rivers and canals provided freight links to major settlements in East Anglia. Stage coaches also radiated out from London to the main towns. The coming of the railway changed this; by 1843 the railway had reached Colchester and by 1845 Norwich, via Cambridge. The railways ended stage coach travel almost immediately, but the canals and navigable rivers were slower to yield to the new competition, with a few still surviving in use.

Coastal shipping and fishing was important, and ports were established at almost all the safe havens on the East Anglian coast. Rail-linked harbours with pretensions to serve the continent at Tollesbury, Aldeburgh and Southwold never developed such links because of navigational problems and the growth of better-situated ports. Even where ports survive today, direct rail freight has been lost at Wells, King's Lynn, Great Yarmouth, Wisbech and Mistley, while at Lowestoft rail traffic is very limited.

Rail links remain at Ipswich and Parkeston Quay, although the Harwich train ferry, important before the Channel Tunnel for rail freight, is no more. Felixstowe, on the other hand, has new rail links to serve the container port, and continental rail passengers are still catered for at Parkeston Quay, now called Harwich International.

East Anglia was also served by a number of long-distance railway links to and from the region. These lines were once particularly important for bringing coal into the area and allowing the prosperous agricultural traffic, together with fish, to be transported elsewhere in Britain. They also provided long-distance links for passengers, travelling to and from East Coast holiday destinations and the port of Harwich. As if almost to reinforce the

FREIGHT SERVICES TO THE CONTINENT

Information and special booklets dealing with the transport of freight to the Continent in
THROUGH WAGONS BY TRAIN FERRY
or in
DOOR TO DOOR CONTAINERS
and by other methods ensuring speed, security and simple documentation are available from:—

Continental Traffic and Shipping Manager,
Harwich House, 129 Bishopsgate, London, E.C.2.
Telephone: Bishopsgate 4702. Telex 25249

Above A train ferry advert, 1964.

serving Great Yarmouth in particular. The line duplicated many of the GER destinations and was an early candidate for closure, with most of the network being closed in February 1959.

The GN&GE line provided a link to Doncaster and the North East. The railway allowed the GNR to access East Anglia from the coal mining areas of Yorkshire, and long-distance freight was once extensive, particularly with coal inwards and agricultural freight outwards. Long-distance passenger 'boat' trains to and from

independence of East Anglia, by the time the railways were nationalised few of the wider links were shown as main lines.

The first of the long-distance rail links to close was the meandering M&GN. As its name suggests, it allowed the Midland and the Great Northern railways to access the Norfolk coast in particular and also Norwich. Holiday traffic was once heavy, and countless summer trains came from the East Midlands. There were also through carriages from destinations further afield, for example Liverpool and Manchester,

Below The steel train ferry gantry landing stage and hinged link span still retains its rails; the earliest example to survive in England, it is listed as an historic structure. The adjoining wooden berthing pier known as 'The Long Arm' also survived in 2013, but demolition has been approved. The view here at Harwich Town was taken in November 2012. *Author*

VIA G.N. & G.E. JOINT RY.

Harwich also used this route, with some through trains travelling as far afield as Scotland.

A southern section of the GN&GE line provided the MR with a link from Kettering, via Huntingdon and St Ives, to Cambridge. Prior to the Second World War there were 13 passenger trains in each direction, but by 1953 this had been reduced to three on weekdays. The southern Huntingdon-St Ives section of the joint line never developed extensive freight traffic and was the first section to close as a through route in June 1959. The joint line north of St Ives to March closed in March 1967, while the March-Spalding section closed as late as November 1982, the last major route to close in the UK.

Links to the Great Northern, Midland and London & North Western railways were provided by the Cambridge-Oxford 'Varsity' line, and these railways all had freight depots at Cambridge. The line's existence had enabled BR to close the Kettering route, and the Cambridge-Oxford line was never proposed for closure in the Beeching Report. Unfortunately the line ran through three BR regions and each took an inconsistent approach to its worth. With some intermediate sections closed, such as Cambridge-Bedford in January 1968, its usefulness as a long-distance link ceased, although there are plans for the reopening of a western section.

Below Class 'D16/3' 4-4-0 No 62578 departs from Melton Constable with a train from the Midlands to Cromer in the summer of 1951. Note the lattice fencing. Melton Constable was once an important railway junction on the M&GN, but the remaining link, via Holt, was recommended for withdrawal in the Beeching Report and closed in 1964. *Ian Allan Library*

This is Cambridge, looking north from Hills Road towards the station, with the LMS Hills Road goods depot on the left and Foster's Mill in the distance. The goods depot marked the most easterly section of the LMS line from Oxford. A newly painted LMS wagon dates this view after 1923, but probably prior to the Second World War. The ex-GER main line remains here, but the ex-LMS lines and sidings have been lost, together with many of the ex-LNER goods lines to the right of this view. *Ian Allan Library*

Above Concrete fencing posts were widely used on the M&GN and together with wooden lattice fencing were a distinctive feature of many M&GN stations. Concrete railway items made at Melton works were a lasting legacy to the skill of the railway's capable manager William Marriott. An original surviving section of fencing is seen here at Melton Constable in August 1994, displaying the high quality of construction. *Author*

Facing page Class 'J15' 0-6-0 No 65432 (note the engine's descending number!) stands at Brightlingsea station. Some locomotives were fitted with side windows for use on this exposed line. The terminus included a station master's house, but was built with a single through platform as original plans to extend the line to St Osyth were never fulfilled. This view was taken on 14 March 1952. *B. Nathan*

Below Capacity problems on the ex-GN&GE Joint Line required sidings to be added at French Drove, north of March. Here Class 20s Nos 20160 and 20136 are seen heading the 08.33 Derby-Yarmouth train on 28 August 1982. The March-Spalding section of the joint line was never recommended for closure in the Beeching Report, but became a very late and short-sighted closure in 1982. *J. Rudd*

3

B-line Essex

Brightlingsea was served by a 5-mile single-line branch from Wivenhoe on the Colchester-Clacton line, which opened in April 1866. There were no intermediate stations and for much of its length the railway ran in an attractive setting on embankments on the eastern flank of the tidal River Colne.

Construction of the harbour at Brightlingsea began at the same time as the railway, but it proved difficult to secure sufficient depth of water for the increasing size of coastal shipping and the harbour work was never completed. However, Brightlingsea became particularly important for oysters and the branch was used to transport barrels of oysters and sprats to Billingsgate. In the 1930s more sprats were landed at Brightlingsea then anywhere else in Britain, and wagon loads were taken from Brightlingsea to the Harwich train ferry for export. Yachts also used the area and tourism developed, with a passenger ferry running between Brightlingsea and Point Clear.

In 1904 there was some flooding of the line, but in 1953 more than 2 miles of the branch were washed away during the February East Coast floods. Such was the scale of devastation that closure was threatened by BR, but the oysters were still being conveyed by train and after a successful fight by the town the line reopened in December of that year. DMUs took over most workings in 1957, the last steam train ran in 1960, and tickets were issued on the train.

Although sometimes shown as a main route on BR maps, the short branch was perhaps inevitably included for closure in the Beeching Report and your author made a trip along the delightful route

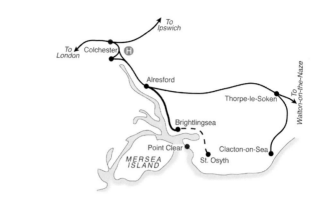

BRIGHTLINGSEA (Essex)

Miles 61¼. Map Sq. 24.
Pop. 4,501. Clos. day Thur.
From Liverpool Street via Wivenhoe.
1st cl.—Single 14/8, Return 27/4.
3rd cl.—Single 9/9, Return 19/6.

Liv. St.	Brightl.	Brightl.	Liv. St.
a.m.		a.m.	
4 35	7 11	6 40r	8 42
8 36e	10 57	7 17sr	9 42
10 36r	12 43	7 17er	9 43
p.m.		8 15sr	9 57
12 30er	2 30	8 17er	9 57
12 36sr	2 20	9 36sr	11 52
2 10e	4 35	11 7er	1 45
2 15s	4 35	p.m.	
3 36r	6 3	1 20sr	4 8
4 56er	6 50	1 20er	4 13
5 36er	7 34	2 40er	4 34
5 36s	7 34	2 40sr	4 46
6 36r	8 40	4 42e	6 39
8 30r	10 17	4 42s	6 48
--	--	6 19ₑ	9 2
—	—	6 38s	9 2
—	—	7 45	9 56
—	—	9 5	12 5

Sunday Trains.

p.m.		p.m.	
4 45	6 45	5 20	7 19
—	—	7 40	10 18
—	—	—	—

e Not Saturday.
r Refreshment Car.
s Saturday only.

Above Departures from
Brightlingsea in April 1956.

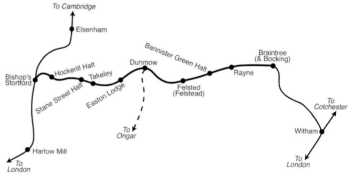

Below A Cravens DMU awaits departure for Colchester on 31 August 1960, at the still gas-lit terminus. Even though this was the height of the summer season, only two coaches were required. The last train, in June 1964, was packed with those wishing to make a final trip on the line. The station was demolished in November 1969 and a community centre now occupies the site. *L. Sandler*

in September 1963. The line, which had a good service and carried commuters to and from London, closed to all traffic, following a further unsuccessful fight by the town, in June 1964. The cost of maintaining the swing bridge at Alresford was said to be the deciding factor in the line's demise.

The station at Brightlingsea had been rebuilt after a fire in 1900 and survived after closure, until it was also partly set on fire in 1968 and demolished the following year. It is possible to walk along much of the route of the railway, which is severed at the site of Alresford swing bridge, although plans for a replacement pedestrian bridge have been considered.

Braintree station remains open with an electric train service to and from Witham, but the 18-mile Braintree-Bishop's Stortford line is closed; the latter once provided a useful link between the London-Colchester and London-Cambridge main lines. The branch was opened in February 1869, but running at right angles to the river valleys in the area it had some steep gradients and a seven-arch viaduct on its route across this undulating part of rural Essex.

A proposed link to Ongar was never built and the line was not a great financial success. Easton Lodge was opened at a level crossing on the line in 1895 for use particularly by King Edward VII, visiting his mistress, the Countess of Warwick, nearby. Hockerill Halt was opened in 1910, and two further halts were added to the line in 1922 to try and generate more passengers in this remote rural area, tickets being issued on the train. At Felstead (as the station was spelled until closure, although the 'a' is now usually omitted) a sugar beet factory was opened in 1926 and supplied its own shunting engines and exchange sidings. The factory once provided heavy seasonal freight for the line and employed almost 300 workers.

The branch was used on occasions as a diversionary route between the two main lines, particularly during the Second World War when air raids had closed one or other of the main lines. Nearby airfields also provided wartime traffic. After the war the branch became less well used and a rival bus service developed along the adjoining main road. Regular passenger services ceased in March 1952, although excursions to Southend and Clacton were run until 1964, together with trains at the beginning and end of term at Felsted School.

Rail freight to Felsted sugar beet factory survived until 1968, some freight to Dunmow until the following year, while remaining freight to a banana warehouse on the line ceased in 1971. A last enthusiasts' passenger train ran in July 1972, although since 1966 the poor structural condition of the seven-arch Langley Viaduct, at Dunmow, had prevented through running, and it was blown up in September 1977. Two miles of track in the western part of the branch were retained until 1974, in the event of the line being required for a new link to Stansted Airport; however, this was not to be and much of the trackbed is now a footpath known as the 'Fitch Way', with a visitor centre at Rayne station.

Below A local passenger train for Witham stands at Takeley station's single platform, headed by Class 'F5' 2-4-2 No 67211, on 10 May 1952. The passing loop, which was authorised for goods trains only, was removed before final closure of this station to coal freight in December 1966. The white-brick station building remains and was cleaned and restored in 2006 by Essex County Council for community use. *T. Rowe*

Below Bishop's Stortford-Braintree timetable, September 1948.

Table 34   BISHOP'S STORTFORD, DUNMOW, and BRAINTREE AND BOCKING

Miles		Week Days only								Miles		Week Days only						
		a.m	a.m	p.m	p.m	p.m	p.m	p.m				a.m	a.m	p.m	p.m	p.m	p.m	p.m
						E	S	E	S							E	S	E	S
—	4 London (L'poolSt) dep	8 20	1150	2 25	4 36	5 0	6 36	7 20	..	—	Braintree & Bocking dep	7 39	10 50	2 0	4 30	4 50	6 35	6 38
—	Bishop's Stortford. dep	9 50	1245	3 26	5 37	5 17	7 35	8 15	..	2¼	Rayne	7 45	10 56	2 6	4 36	4 56	6 41	6 44
1¾	Hockerill Halt.	9 54	1249	3 30	5 41	5 5b	7 39	8 19	..	4	Bannister Green Halt...	7 49	11 0	2 10	4 40	5 0	6 45	6 48
4	Stane Street Halt	10 0	1255	3 36	5 47	6 1 7	45 8	25	..	6¼	Felstead for Little Dun-	7 54	11 6	2 15	4 46	5 6	6 50	6 53
5¾	Takeley	10 4	1259	3 40	5 51	6 5 7	49 8	29	..	8¼	Dunmow ....[mow	8 2	11 14	2 22	4 54	5 14	6 57	7 0
7¾	Easton Lodge	10 9		4 3	4 55	5 56	6 10	7 54	8 34	10¼	Easton Lodge	8 8	11 20	2 28	5 0	5 20	7 3	7 6
9¼	Dunmow ......[mow	1015	1 10	3 50	6 3	6 15	8 1	8 41	..	12¼	Takeley	8 13	11 25	2 33	5 5	5 25	7 8	7 11
11¼	Felstead for Little Dun..	1022	1 16	3 56	6 9	6 21	8 7	8 47	..	14	Stane Street Halt	8 16	11 28	2 36	5 5	5 28	7 11	7 14
13¼	Bannister Green Halt...	1027	1 20	4 1	6 14	6 26	8 12	8 52	..	16¼	Hockerill Halt.	8 22	11 34	2 42	5 14	5 34	7 17	..
15¼	Rayne	1033	1 26	4 7	6 20	6 32	8 18	8 58	..	18	Bishop's Stortford. arr	8 25	11 37	2 45	5 17	5 37	7 20	7 21
18	Braintree & Bocking arr	1038	1 31	4 12	6 25	6 37	8 24	9 4	..	48¾	4 London(L'poolSt) arr	9 23	1237.5	6 0	6 48	6 48	8 45	8 45

B Arr. 5 3 p.m. on Saturdays
E Except Saturdays
N Arr. 12 45 p.m. on Saturdays

S Saturdays only

Tickets from the Halts and Easton Lodge issued on train

Passengers to or from Stane Street and Bannister Green Halts must travel in special car provided

Left Just beyond Braintree station the line became increasingly overgrown after closure and is seen here in the summer of 1980. However, in 1994 the footpath was widened and surfaced as part of the Braintree-Bishop's Stortford long-distance 'Fitch Way' footpath. The overbridge was also altered, but the gradient post in the left foreground remained in September 2012. *Author*

Left A cast-iron fingerpost at Dunmow remarkably still indicated the LNER station in October 1980, when this view was taken. This was more than a decade after the station had finally closed in April 1969, and more than 30 years since the LNER had ceased as an organisation. The sign was made at the Maldon Iron Works and survived in 2012, although the station sign itself had been removed and placed in Dunmow museum. *Author*

4

The 'Crab and Winkle' line

As the network of secondary railway lines grew, there was disquiet that there were no railways serving the remote agricultural area between the Blackwater and Colne rivers, to the east of the London-Colchester main line. It was considered that the settlements, businesses and fruit farms in this area were disadvantaged because of their distance from the nearest railway.

Consequently a light railway was proposed from Kelvedon to Tollesbury and on to the coast at Tollesbury Pier. Here in remote marshland a substantial 1,770-foot (540-metre) wooden pier was built out over the mud to reach the deeper waters of the Blackwater estuary. The ambitious aim of the pier was for it to become the basis of a continental ferry port, but also a calling point for East Coast paddle boats and the centre of a yachting resort, with seaside properties to rival Burnham-on-Crouch.

The Kelvedon Low Level-Tollesbury section opened in October 1904; it was worked by the GER and was conductor-guard-operated from the outset. In May 1905 the line was extended to Tollesbury Pier, giving a total length of 10¼ miles of light railway, excluding sidings to farms on the route. The First World War saw the pier being used for troop training, but this did little to promote greater links with the continent.

Shellfish from the Blackwater estuary gave the line its local nickname, the 'Crab and Winkle'. At its

Table 22   KELVEDON and TOLLESBURY (Light Railway)—(One class only)

Miles		Week Days only					Miles			Week Days only			
		a.m	p.m							a.m	p.m	p.m	
—	Kelvedon ...... dep	1010	.. 5 45	..	..	..	—	Tollesbury ..... dep	8 30	..	1250	.. 6 37	Tickets (single only) and Local Tickets are issued on the train
½	Feering Halt........	1013	.. 5 48	..	..	..	2	Tolleshunt D'Arcy..	8 38	..	1 5	.. 6 50	
2¼	Inworth	1020	.. 5 55	..	..	..	4½	Tolleshunt Knights..	8 44	..	1 11	.. 6 56	
3½	Tiptree	1029	.. 6 4	..	..	..	5	Tiptree	8 54	..	1 35	.. 7 7	
4	Tolleshunt Knights.	1033	.. 6 8	..	..	..	5½	Inworth	8 57	..	1 38	.. 7 10	
6½	Tolleshunt D'Arcy ..	1045	.. 6 20	..	..	..	8	Feering Halt	9 5	..	1 46	.. 7 18	
8½	Tollesbury ..... arr	1050	.. 6 25	..	..	..	8½	Kelvedon .... arr	9 9	..	1 50	.. 7 22	

Above The timetable for September 1948.

Facing page This is Kelvedon Low Level station on 17 September 1949. The single platform and small wooden waiting shelter were accessed by a covered footbridge, running from the main-line station over a local road and the River Blackwater. This picturesque station closed to passengers in May 1951. *R. E. Vincent*

Below A mixed train arrives at Kelvedon Low Level, also on 17 September 1949, headed by Class 'J69' 0-6-0T No 68578. The coaches are interesting; that nearest the engine is an ex-GER six-wheeler especially adapted with steps for use with the low platforms on the line. The second coach is an ex-Wisbech & Upwell Tramway gas-lit bogie car, which was transferred to the line in 1928. The conductor guard issued tickets on the train. *R. E. Vincent*

peak more than 100,000 oysters were transported along the line in a single day. Agricultural freight traffic also developed on the railway, but the pier section never met expectations, in part because of silting up of the Blackwater estuary, but also because the isolated and marshy location did not attract much interest. In July 1921 the Pier station closed to all traffic, having been in operation for just 14 years. For a time after its closure this section of line was used for the storage of rolling stock.

During the Second World War the War Department made use of the pier line beyond Tollesbury as part of the defences to prevent a coastal

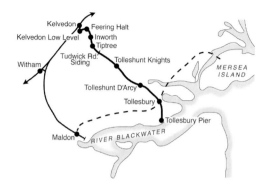

main section of line was busy with six up and seven down timetabled trains daily.

By the time the railways were nationalised, in 1948, rival bus services were making inroads into the railway's finances. An infrequent service of two up and three down trains, together with slow journeys, including mixed trains averaging just 8.5mph, resulted in ever fewer numbers using the railway. At one time more than 1,000 passengers had used the line on busy summer Saturdays, but soon after BR had taken over the numbers had reduced to fewer than 100 a day. Little objection was raised to the withdrawal of passenger services, and the last passenger train ran on 5 May 1951, when large crowds came to say goodbye.

invasion, and a rail-mounted mobile gun patrolled this section. However, the track and decking on the pier itself was removed and a section deliberately blown up as a counter-invasion measure.

The Wilkin & Sons jam-making factory at Tiptree became the most important freight user of the line. Fruit was delivered and thousands of jars of jam found their way from Tiptree to customers throughout the country. Staff working at the jam factory also used the line, together with summer fruit-pickers. Prior to the Second World War the

Below This is Feering Halt, with newly painted crossing gates and posts, open to the A12 trunk road, looking towards Kelvedon station in March 1957, after closure to regular passenger traffic. The light railway did provide several level crossing gates, and at Tolleshunt D'Arcy the crossing-keeper's house still remains. Feering Halt was opened by the LNER in 1934. The Distant signal beyond the gates had a fixed arm, the only operational signalling being at Kelvedon. *H. Davies*

After closure to passengers all traffic ceased beyond Tudwick Road Siding, which was used for fruit collection, in October 1951. The track towards Tollesbury was soon taken up and most remains of the pier demolished. With a reduction in coal freight and with the jam factory at Tiptree gradually transferring to road transport, the remaining section of line closed in October 1962.

After the last freight train the track was removed and most of the surviving station buildings were demolished. The light railway had few major earthworks and just one bridge, but for many years sections were clearly visible in the countryside. Today fewer and fewer remnants are to be seen as the line has been built upon, or much of the trackbed returned to agriculture. The Tiptree jam factory remains and contains a museum with a small section devoted to the railway.

Below The wooden buildings at Tiptree station, seen in March 1957, still remained at that time, acting as a freight office after passenger services had been withdrawn in May 1951. By 1961 Wilkin & Sons' jam traffic had been transferred to road transport and little or no rail freight was handled here. *H. Davies*

Facing page top The Railway Enthusiasts' Club ran a special train headed by Class 'J15' 0-6-0 No 65443 on 6 April 1957, seen here at Tiptree. The locomotive was based at Colchester shed and was scrapped in 1960. Note the ladders used to disembark from the wagons, in an era before 'health and safety' rules would prohibit such practices. *H. Davies*

Facing page bottom Tollesbury station is seen in 1950 from the ungated level crossing, looking towards Kelvedon. A speed restriction of 10mph was imposed at such road crossings on the line. The LNER poster hoarding headings had still to be replaced with those of BR. The station acted as the terminus of the line after the extension to the pier closed in 1921. An earlier proposal for a Maldon-Mersea line, via Tollesbury, had never been realised. *Ian Allan Library*

Above Tollesbury Pier became unusable after being blown up in 1940. Note the Second World War pillbox at its entrance – all part of anti-invasion measures. The remaining sections of the 1,770-foot (540-metre) wooden pier were demolished in 1951, but some wooden palisading at the foot of the adjoining embankment still survived in 2013. In the background a laid-up American Second World War 'Liberty' cargo ship is to be noted. *C. Footer*

Below This is part of the site of Kelvedon Low Level station, the western terminus of the light railway, in March 2012. Although all the buildings have long been demolished, much of the now heavily overgrown Low Level station and some sleepers to retain the embankment remain. The station site is visible beside the main London-Norwich line, which is carried on the viaduct in the foreground. *Author*

5

The 'Gin and Toffee' line

The 5½-mile Elsenham & Thaxted Light Railway was the last branch line built in East Anglia, the later and shorter Stansted Airport and Felixstowe Dock links excepted. The railway was locally promoted to help relieve agricultural poverty in a remote part of north-west Essex and to support the market town of Thaxted, which had declined from a settlement of some importance.

The line was originally intended as a narrow-gauge railway extending to Great Bardfield. It had been sanctioned in 1906, but did not open until April 1913, as there were difficulties in raising capital and the GER was unhappy about working a narrow-gauge line. In the end government money was provided and local capital was forthcoming from Sir William Gilbey, owner of a firm making gin and other drinks, who lived at Elsenham Hall, together with George Lee, a confectionary manufacturer and the main employer in Thaxted. The involvement of

these two entrepreneurs gave the railway its local 'Gin and Toffee' nickname. In the end a standard-gauge light railway opened with no signalling, or crossing gates; speed was limited to 25mph, apart from at level crossings, where it was reduced to 10mph.

The single line was built with economy in mind. At Thaxted the station was located in an isolated area some way from the town centre, in order to save money constructing earthworks and a bridge over the River Chelmer. In fact, there was only one bridge on the entire line. Sibley's for Chickney & Broxted

Facing page The 2.28pm Thaxted train leaves Elsenham on 12 September 1952, a day before the passenger service was withdrawn. The train is approaching the junction for the north curve, which provided a connection to the main line via the goods yard. *P. Bray*

Below Class 'J69' 0-6-0T No 68609 heads the 11.50am Thaxted-Elsenham train on 18 August 1951. The view is between Henham and Mill Road halts; the latter was added in 1922, and made the two halts less than a mile apart. It is not difficult from this rural agricultural view to understand why this branch was known as one of the East Anglian 'Farmers' Lines'. *Ian Allan Library*

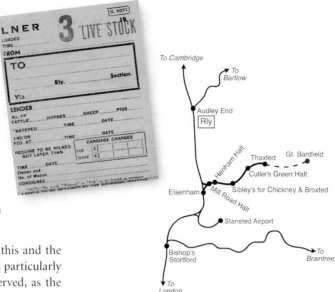

was the only intermediate station, and this and the three other halts on the line were not all particularly well located for the settlements they served, as the light railway followed the contours to save on construction costs. Cutler's Green Halt was unique in having no road connection at all, being accessed only by local footpaths.

The line was well used for freight during the First World War, when agricultural output was boosted to offset the loss of imported goods. The 1920s and 1930s saw passenger traffic receipts generally sustained, with some tourists and ramblers adding to local use. There was no competing bus service and Mill Road Halt was opened by the GER in 1922.

In spite of all this the line was not a great overall commercial success. The inconveniently located stations, the slow mixed trains taking almost half an hour for the 5½-mile journey, and the absence of through trains and through tickets – all tickets were issued by the conductor guard – resulted in buses increasingly taking over passenger traffic.

The railway never really recovered from the cut in passenger services during the Second World War and was one of the first candidates for closure when

BR took over. The line closed in September 1952 to passengers, when many travelled on the last day to say farewell. In June of the following year the line also closed for freight. The lifting of petrol rationing had already allowed George Lee to transfer his confectionary deliveries to Leyland lorries.

The railway was one of the last to open and first to close after a relatively short life of just under 50 years. It was lightly built and much of the route has been returned to agriculture. However, the wooden waiting room, together with the engine shed and water tower, survives at Thaxted.

George Lee's toffee business closed in 1969 and Gilbey's gin business ceased its UK operations in 1985. The attractive Elsenham station, on the main London-Cambridge line remains open.

Below The timetable for September 1948.

Bottom Class 'J69' 0-6-0T No 68530 heads the 11.50am Thaxted-Elsenham train at Henham Halt on 6 August 1951. Note the old carriage used as a shelter and office, a feature of several East Anglian halts. Few remains are to be found here today. *Ian Allan Library*

ELSENHAM and THAXTED (Light Railway)

Table 35

[Timetable — Week Days only]

One class only between Elsenham and Thaxted.

B Third class only between Elsenham and Bishop's Stortford. E Except Saturdays. F Dep. 3 42 p.m on Saturdays.
S Saturdays only. Tickets (single only) issued on the train.

Above As light railways were built to save on costs, Thaxted station was located some considerable way to the south-west of the town in a remote rural area, as demonstrated by this scene looking from the end of the line in 1936. The importance of the railway for local deliveries of coal is also well illustrated in this view. The highest point on the whole of the GER was reached west of Thaxted station. *Ian Allan Library*

Below No 68530 is seen again at Thaxted station, this time on 30 June 1951. The two coaches were originally built for wartime ambulance work; modified for conductor guard working, they were supplied to the line in 1948. There was only one class in the coaches and only single tickets were issued. *H. C. Casserley*

Above Thaxted station is seen in March 2012, almost 60 years since closure to passengers. The purpose-built wooden passenger building has survived with its fading green and cream paintwork and is now in the grounds of a residential property in the former station area. *Author*

Right The brick water tower and single-road engine shed at Thaxted still survive and are seen here in March 2012. The engine shed was a sub-shed of Cambridge (31A) and is one of the few sheds to survive. East Anglia's light railways were on the whole lightly built, but these buildings were the most substantial structures on the line and some of the last to be built by the GER. *Author*

6

CVH 2-4-2T No 2 *Halstead* was built by Hawthorn Leslie in 1887. This view is undated, but the locomotive has the long stovepipe chimney as originally fitted, before being rebuilt at Stratford Works in 1896. It is seen here at Yeldham, hauling a rake of assorted mainly six-wheeled coaches. *Ian Allan Library*

Strangers within the gates

The Colne Valley & Halstead Railway was a single line that opened from Chappel Junction to a temporary station at Halstead in April 1860. It had been extended to Haverhill by May 1863, providing a 19-mile highly individual railway following the River Colne for much of its route. Halstead, a town once renowned for its silk weaving and at the heart of a fruit-growing area, became the centre of the railway, while bricks from local works were also conveyed on the line.

Working relations with other railways were less than cordial at first, and this provoked the CVH into considering extending its line to Cambridge and Colchester, destinations already served by what was to become the GER. In the end pragmatism and the early financial difficulties of the small independent railway, which prevented it from owning its own locomotive until 1876, prevailed, and the planned lines were never built. In fact, the CVH carriages were hauled behind GER trains to and from Marks Tey, and CVH locomotives were serviced at Stratford.

Largely because of the poor financial state of the railway, it never became part of the GER and remained independent until the LNER took over the ailing company in 1923. Rationalisations and improvements were soon implemented. The LNER closed the head office and running shed at Halstead and diverted passenger services from Haverhill South to the former GER station in the town. Track was relaid, old passenger stock scrapped and signalling updated.

The five locomotives owned by the railway also passed to the LNER. No 1, an 0-4-2T built by Neilson, was in a derelict condition and was scrapped in 1923. There were three 2-4-2Ts, all built by Hawthorn Leslie: No 2 *Halstead* became LNER No 8312 and was scrapped in 1930; No 3 *Colne* became LNER No 8313 and survived until 1927; and No 4 *Hedingham* was scrapped in 1923 before receiving a new LNER number. No 5, an 0-6-2T built by Hudswell Clark, became LNER No 8314 and was withdrawn in 1928.

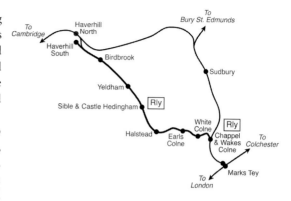

Below Colne Valley & Halstead Railway 0-4-2T No 1 was built by Neilson & Co in 1876, and is seen here as rebuilt to a Johnson design by Hawthorn Leslie in 1885. The supplementary water tanks at the front of the locomotive were added in 1888 and removed in 1911, giving the time period of this undated view. This was the oldest engine on the line and, being in unserviceable condition, was scrapped when the LNER took over in 1923. *Ian Allan Library*

The superiority of the Long Melford line prevented the development of widespread Colchester-Cambridge through workings via Halstead. Although the CVH route was 6 miles shorter, gradients were as steep as 1 in 60, while some speed and weight restrictions remained. Nonetheless, LNER rationalisations ensured that several Cambridge-Colchester trains used the shorter route. The Second World War saw busy use of the line, particularly associated with the air bases in the area, while fruit, coal and the brickworks all continued to provide freight.

In 1959 DMUs were introduced, there were commuters to London, and some through Halstead-

Above No 2 is seen again with its later copper-capped chimney. Note the large abbreviated 'CV' initials on the tank side, rather than the full CV&HR title, when this undated pre-1923 view was taken at Halstead. The locomotive survived to become LNER Class 'F9' No 8312 and lasted until 1930. *Ian Allan Library*

Below CVH 2-4-2T No 3 *Colne*, dating from 1887 and also built by Hawthorn Leslie, heads a Haverhill-Chappel train at Colne Valley Junction. The junction signal box was closed by the LNER in 1925 and was demolished in 1927. The locomotive was absorbed into the LNER, becoming Class 'F9' No 8313, and survived until December 1927. *K. Nunn*

Colchester services were provided, but savings were insufficient to save the line and it closed to passengers in December 1961. A freight service was maintained south of Yeldham until December 1964, when it was cut back to Halstead. This remaining southern section, together with Haverhill South, closed in April 1965.

Below CVH 2-4-2T No 4 *Hedingham*, built by Hawthorn Leslie in 1894, is seen at Haverhill goods yard on 29 July 1911. The locomotive had been rebuilt at Stratford Works in 1902, but was not taken into LNER operating stock, being withdrawn in 1923. *LPC*

In March 1967 your author walked from Castle Hedingham to Halstead. The track had been removed in 1966, but crossing gate lamps, mileposts and even a signal post, complete with signal arm, remained at that time. However, some metal bridges had already been removed and my diary records that I was forced to wade across a river – I was young at the time!

In 1975 steam trains returned to Castle Hedingham, which became the centre of the Colne Valley Railway, a heritage centre with much stock and plans to extend the line to Yeldham.

Bottom CVH 0-6-2T No 5, the most modern locomotive on the line, was built by Hudswell Clark to a Hawkins design in 1908. The original wrought- and cast-iron bridges had to be strengthened for the locomotive to run on the line. Note the full initials 'CV&HR' on the tank. The view here is at Halstead on 29 July 1911. The engine became LNER Class 'N18' No 8314 and worked on the Brightlingsea line for a time, before being withdrawn in 1928. *Ian Allan Library*

Right The former CVR 2-4-2T No 2, previously *Halstead*, is seen here as LNER Class 'F9' No 8312 and out of use awaiting scrapping, soon after its withdrawal in 1930. When the LNER took over the ex-CVR locomotives on the line they were gradually replaced, particularly by ex-GER locomotives. *Ian Allan Library*

Left Seen from the guard's van of a freight train, Ivatt Class 2 2-6-0 No 46466 heads a train about to pass Sible & Castle Hedingham station. Note the industry that grew around some of the rural stations along the line. The station building was dismantled after closure of the line and re-erected on the preserved Colne Valley Railway. The locomotive was allocated to Cambridge shed as new in 1951 and was withdrawn in 1962, giving the time period for this view. *D. Lawrence*

Left A freight train hauled by a BTH Type 1 diesel enters White Colne station. Note the old coach that had been used as a waiting room. This diesel locomotive was introduced in 1957, and the remaining freight ceased on this section of line in 1965, giving a time period for this view. The main station building at White Colne still survives and is used as the village hall. *D. Lawrence*

7

Stour Valley sabotage

The 43-mile Shelford-Marks Tey line was a secondary route, but served a rich agricultural area and later the expanding towns of Sudbury and Haverhill. It also functioned as a useful alternative to the main lines for long-distance trains to and from the Essex coast. At closure there still remained five crossing points to allow for heavy use of the single line.

During the Second World War, particularly because of air bases in the area, the route was extremely busy and operated throughout the night. Bomb and supply trains used the line, while the aviation fuel tanks at Chappel & Wakes Colne received hundreds of petrol trains. After the war, non-stop and limited-stop summer-only passenger services were reintroduced by BR and used the line as part of a Leicester-Clacton service in particular. In 1959 DMUs took over most local passenger services.

On the freight side, coal and local agricultural produce were among the main flows on the line, but some long-distance Whitemoor-Colchester freight services also used it. In 1963 BR indicated that freight services were secure for 'twenty years', although freight services south from Sudbury ceased in November of the following year and to the north of Sudbury in October 1966. Many smaller intermediate stations had already closed to freight by this time, while Colchester-Halstead freight used the Chappel-Marks Tey section of the line until April 1965.

The line was identified for closure in the Beeching Report. In 1966 all remaining booking offices were closed and single tickets for branch stations only were issued on the train. This required passengers to rebook for all other destinations, even though the conductor guard's ticket machines could issue through and return tickets. The timetable, which was not even displayed at a number of stations, also gave several poor connections at Marks Tey and entailed some through trains along the line waiting for up to 1½ hours at Sudbury, making day trips to Cambridge unattractive. New restrictions on the use of tickets from London were also introduced for passengers using the branch.

There was outrage at BR's management, which put an embargo on its statistics in relation to the route after one set of figures showed the line making a profit. Constructive suggestions for reducing crossing stations were put forward, together with a new timetable with better connections. It was pointed out that the line served the expanding towns of Haverhill and Sudbury and therefore had the potential for increased viability, but BR remained stubbornly committed to closure.

Facing page At Long Melford the 10.50am Clacton-on-Sea to Leicester train, headed by Class 'B12/3' 4-6-0 No 61576, passes through the station while the 8.14am Leicester to Clacton-on-Sea train is waiting at the signal headed by sister Class 'B12/3' No 61561 on Saturday 19 July 1958. *G. Mortimer*

Below The Stour Valley and Long Melford-Bury timetable, September 1948.

Table 23

MARK'S TEY, SUDBURY, BURY ST. EDMUNDS, HAVERHILL (North) and CAMBRIDGE

[Timetable image — Table 23. A detailed multi-column railway timetable with columns for Week Days and Sundays, showing stations: London (L'poolSt) dep, Colchester, Mark's Tey dep, Chappel & Wakes Colne, Bures, Sudbury (Suffolk) arr/dep, Long Melford arr/dep, Lavenham, Cockfield (Suffolk), Welnetham, Bury St. Edmunds arr, Long Melford dep, Glemsford, Cavendish, Clare, Stoke (Suffolk), Sturmer, Haverhill (North), Bartlow arr/dep, London (L'poolSt) arr, Linton, Pampisford, Shelford, Cambridge arr, London (L'poolSt) arr]

Arr. 4 minutes *earlier*   S Saturdays only   Z Arr. 5 3 p.m. on Saturdays

For **OTHER TRAINS** between Shelford and Cambridge, see Table 4

The local authorities in the area even agreed to finance the line to keep it open, but out of the blue the BR management doubled the costs involved. After a vigorous fight, closure north of Sudbury was finally implemented in March 1967, but not before a girder bridge was expensively replaced on this section. The line north of Sudbury was closed amidst much controversy and anger at the shameful behaviour of BR, which was accused in the press of having 'a plot to destroy the traffic and so close the line'. The Marks Tey-Sudbury section was retained, and further efforts by BR to close this section were made right up to 1974, when the fuel crisis effectively put an end to further closures.

After the last trains ran, the railway land was sold off in a piecemeal manner, making reopening difficult. Today reminders of the line can be found all along the route, while its history can be discovered at Clare station, which is part of a country park, and at the East Anglian Railway Museum at Chappel & Wakes Colne station on the surviving Marks Tey-Sudbury section. In the first five years after privatisation passengers on the remaining line increased by 76% and there have been calls for the Haverhill-Cambridge section to reopen.

Below At Rodbridge level crossing near Long Melford the gates are being closed to trains on 3 December 1966. The gate lamp case on the right is of an LNER lightweight pattern, as opposed to the more traditional LNER cast-iron lamp case on the gate being closed. *G. Mortimer*

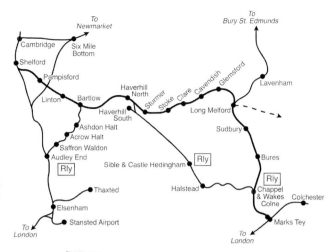

Below The 7.26am Leicester London Road to Clacton-on-Sea through train climbs Bartlow Bank hauled by Brush Type 2 No D5621 on 22 August 1964. The second coach of this six-coach train, behind a BR Mark 1 example, is an ex-LNER teak-bodied vehicle. Excursions over the line to the coast were first introduced by the GER. *G. Mortimer*

Left The single-line token is exchanged at Haverhill between the signalman and the driver of the 10.55am Cambridge-Sudbury DMU service on 18 February 1967. The fact that trains only ran as far as Sudbury at this time and did not continue through to Colchester reduced passenger numbers using the line. *G. Mortimer*

Below A DMU forming the 12.30pm Sudbury-Cambridge service approaches Haverhill station on 21 January 1967. The goods shed can be seen bottom left. By this time the rumours of closure had been confirmed – it was to take place in March.
G. Mortimer

Above The 1.47pm Cambridge-Sudbury train calls at Cavendish station on 4 March 1967, decorated with bunting to mark the last day of services. Today only the station crossing-keeper's house and a short section of platform remain. *G. Mortimer*

Left This is the disused Clare station in November 2012; the station master's two-storey house is to the left. Built in red brick with white brick dressings, the building survives as part of Clare Country Park. A display about the railway is provided in the former goods shed, which houses a goods van. The platform buildings also survive. *Author*

Right Bartlow was the junction station for the Saffron Walden branch. The main station building had been well restored and imaginatively named as 'Booking Hall' when this view was taken in June 2012. Many stations on the line were built to a characteristic GER architectural style. However, there were many variations, such as this example, built in white brick, when most on the line were built of red brick with white-brick dressings. *Author*

8

Change at Bentley for Hadleigh

The main line north of Colchester was originally proposed to run through Hadleigh and on to Bury St Edmunds, but this proposal was abandoned in favour of a route via the larger port of Ipswich. Nevertheless Hadleigh was an important market town with milling, malting and manufacturing, and businessmen here were keen to be connected to the railway network. As a consequence a branch off the Colchester-Ipswich line was promoted, and in August 1847 there were great celebrations at Hadleigh as the first train arrived, with the line opening to regular traffic the following month.

It was envisaged that the 7½-mile Bentley Junction-Hadleigh single line would form part of a longer link from Harwich to the Midlands. In 1901 a light railway extension westward to Long Melford was proposed, but Hadleigh was to remain the railhead. A two-way triangular junction was provided with the main line at Bentley Junction, and the branch was built to

provide for eventual double track if required. It was well-constructed with gentle gradients and curves, together with long straight sections. Consequently good turns of speed were not unknown, particularly where there were no level crossings.

At the opening of the branch the station buildings were not complete, but when eventually finished

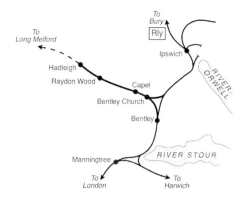

Facing page Bentley station, on the London-Norwich main line, was the junction for the Hadleigh branch, and is seen here with a Felixstowe Beach-Liverpool Street train passing through, headed by Class 'B12/3' 4-6-0 No 61570, on 7 June 1949. The single line to Hadleigh can be seen on the left; it ran beside the main line from Bentley station for more than half a mile before veering westward to Hadleigh. Bentley station closed in November 1966. *G. Mortimer*

Below The elegant terminus at Hadleigh reflected the civic pride in the railway reaching the town. When this view was taken on 30 September 1956 the building was no longer used for passenger purposes, but was still operational as a freight office; it survives today as an attractive dwelling. The large industrial building in the background has also been replaced by residential development. *D. Lawrence*

they were both flamboyant and impressive. Built to a Victorian mix of Georgian and Italianate styles, including attractive Venetian-style windows and imposing tall chimney stacks, they were constructed in a mix of red and white bricks. All were built to individual designs, but all were clearly related in architectural style, including the tiny crossing-keeper's cottage at Bentley Church Road.

Excursions from the branch to London and Yarmouth were among those occasionally provided, but regular passenger traffic was not heavy. The remote station at Bentley Church Road was closed as early as December 1853. The northern spur from the branch, which provided a direct link to Ipswich, was used as a siding until it was also closed in 1875. After that time any through Hadleigh-Ipswich market-day trains had to reverse at Bentley Junction, but most branch passenger services terminated there. In 1876 a slip coach for Hadleigh was detached at Bentley Junction, but this was withdrawn the following year.

Conductor guards were introduced on the branch in 1922, but the line succumbed early, particularly to direct Hadleigh-Ipswich buses, closing to passengers in February 1932. There was subsequently an illustrious passenger train in 1956, when the Royal Train was stabled on the branch overnight to ensure a

BENTLEY and HADLEIGH.—Great Eastern.

Down.		Week Days.									Up.			Week Days.						
Miles		mrn	mrn	mrn	aft	aft	aft	aft			Miles		mrn	mrn	aft	aft	aft	aft	aft	
	Liverpool Street, 258 London...dep.	5 6	5 43	11 45	2 22	3 32	3 32	5 30				Hadleigh .....dep.	7 55	9 16	1 10	2 58	5 35	6 54	7 0	
2¼	Bentley ......dep.	8 33	9 46	1 50	5 8	6 20	6 27	7 27			2¼	Raydon Wood....	8 09	9 21	1 15	3 3	5 42	6 59	7 6	
2¼	Capel.............	8 40	9 52	1 56	5 14	6 26	6 33	7 33			5	Capel.............	8 09	9 28	1 22	3 10	5 52	7 6	7 12	
5	Raydon Wood.....	8 49	9 59	2 3	5 21	6 33	6 40	7 40			7¼	Bentley 268, 292.	8 12	9 34	1 28	3 16	6 0	7 12	7 18	
7¼	Hadleigh .....arr.	8 56	10 52	9 5	5 27	6 39	6 46	7 46			70¼	292 London*.. arr.	10 26		3 30		8 a5			

*a Arrives at 8 15 aft. on Saturdays.   * Liverpool Street Station.*

Above The timetable for April 1910.

quiet night's sleep for a member of the Royal Family. Occasional special passenger trains were also run.

Freight continued, and during the Second World War the branch was particularly busy serving the air base at Raydon. At first construction material arrived at Raydon Wood station to build the airfield, then in due course disassembled aircraft were also delivered by rail. A siding was built to munitions stores in Raydon Wood, while further munitions stores provided freight for the line near Hadleigh.

After the war coal and agricultural produce became the mainstay of the branch, and as a consequence freight services ran until April 1965. Bentley station survived for passengers until November 1966, freight having ceased at the junction station in 1964. The last train to call at Bentley was celebrated by few, your author purchasing the last ticket.

Today the station buildings at Hadleigh, Raydon Wood and Bentley, together with the crossing-keeper's cottage at Bentley Church Road, survive.

Capel was demolished to make way for the dualling of the A12, while the Hadleigh Railway Walk uses the branch trackbed between Raydon and Hadleigh.

Below The road level crossing at Raydon Wood station was operated by the train crew. It is seen here on 5 March 1965 from the platform end with a freight train, hauled by Brush Type 2 No D5636, waiting to cross the road. *H. James*

Right The 12.30 Ipswich-Hadleigh freight hurries along near Raydon Wood headed by Brush Type 2 No D5699 on 13 April 1965, just two days before closure of the branch. Bridges along the line were built for possible double track, but it remained single track throughout its lifetime, and plans to extend the line beyond Hadleigh never materialised. *G. Mortimer*

Below The final train service from Hadleigh, the 16.10 freight to Ipswich on 15 April 1965, leaves Hadleigh station. The train, drawn by Brush Type 2 No D5699, was watched by a few enthusiasts, in contrast to the arrival of the opening train on 21 August 1847 when 'bells were rung and guns boomed in all directions'. *G. Mortimer*

G. E. R.

From

TO

HADLEIGH

Left The side elevation of Raydon Wood station is seen in March 2012. The listed building, constructed in Suffolk red brick with white brick decoration, was undergoing a refurbishment when this view was taken. The platform railings and a lamp standard also remain. The station was located some considerable distance to the north of the village of Raydon itself, indicating the importance of agricultural freight rather than passenger traffic at this location. *Author*

Below The Hadleigh Railway Walk uses a section of the Hadleigh-Raydon Wood trackbed just over 2 miles long. The well-used public right of way is seen here on the embankment near the Hook Lane overbridge in April 2013. *Author*

Facing page A Class 'J70' 0-6-0T tram engine with BR lettering shunts at Ipswich Docks on 21 September 1950. The last two remaining steam dock trams at Ipswich were withdrawn and replaced by diesel shunting engines in 1954. *Mrs Dimbleby*

9

The Ipswich Docks branch

A new dock with locks that enabled ships to load and unload at all states of the tide was opened at Ipswich in 1842 and at the time was the largest in Britain. The new dock, known as the Wet Dock, involved diversion of the River Orwell along what was called the New Cut. The railway arrived at Ipswich a few years later, in 1846, and rails were provided to the Griffin Wharf area on the west bank of the River Orwell, on the opposite side of the river from the new dock, which remained unconnected to the railway network.

The issue was resolved after the railway was extended through Ipswich Tunnel to the site of the present station. Freight facilities were developed with the opening of a new branch from Ipswich Upper Yard to Ipswich Lower Yard in 1866, together with an extension of this branch to link with tramways serving the Wet Dock area.

The docks branch line included a weak bridge over the River Gipping between the Upper and Lower yards and, although a substantial central steel support was provided, the bridge was to limit for all time the weight of locomotives that could access the main dock area. The line to Griffin Wharf continued to serve the western bank of the River Orwell.

In 1877 further dock improvements began that allowed dockside trams to operate along the entire length of the 'Island' between the New Cut and the Wet Dock. Various additional tramways were proposed in 1913, which allowed direct ship-to-railway transfer at most quays in the dock area and also provided flexibility in working the busy lines. The advent of the First World War delayed this development, but the tramway network was completed after the war.

Although the docks were mainly used for freight, regular passenger excursions were run by paddle steamers from Ipswich to coastal resorts and London. Such were the steamer passenger numbers prior to the First World War that the tramways and railways serving the docks were considered for passenger use.

Below A map of the Ipswich Docks branch in 1928.
Crown Copyright

The quayside tramways had both a restricted axle weight and sharp curves, resulting in the use of tram engines with light axle loads and short wheelbases. The first two of the new Class 'J70' 0-6-0T tram engines, built at Stratford Works, Nos 135 and 136 of 1903, were allocated to Ipswich Docks. At their peak up to six tram engines were used on the dock tramways and connecting lines, and the dock network, with its grain, timber, livestock, fertiliser and coal traffic together with other minerals and general freight, was once very busy.

There was a gradual decline in the amount of rail freight using the dock lines after the Second World War. By 1954 only two steam tram engines remained, and Drewry diesel shunters replaced them in that year. By the early 1990s most sections had fallen out of use, but much track remained. The last working over the dock branch was in November 2006. Redevelopment of part of the dockside waterfront has seen quayside

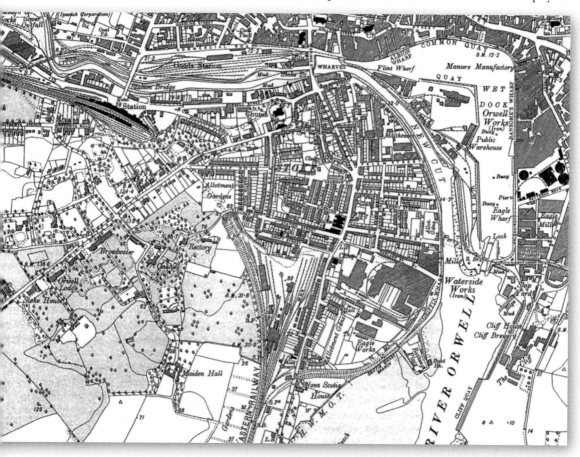

tramway track removed from this part of the Wet Dock, but the connecting dock branch was not officially closed until February 2009. The branch was cut at Stoke Bridge in April 2010 and further sections of track and remaining sidings were removed in the area of the former Lower Yard in 2011.

In March 2012 the rusting and overgrown track from the Upper Yard to the entrance of the Lower Yard was formally closed. Isolated and disused sections of dockside tramway could still be found throughout

the dock complex in 2013. The truncated Halifax Junction-Griffin Wharf line is still available for rail freight serving an operational area of Ipswich Docks.

Below Class 'J70' 0-6-0T tram engine No 68216, designed by James Holden and dating from 1903, is seen on 30 August 1951 at Ipswich Docks. It is passing under a conveyor for grain that was exported from the dock. The sweltering cab conditions in hot weather were improved by opening the front and rear doors. The tram engine was withdrawn in 1953 and scrapped at Stratford shed. *Ian Allan Library*

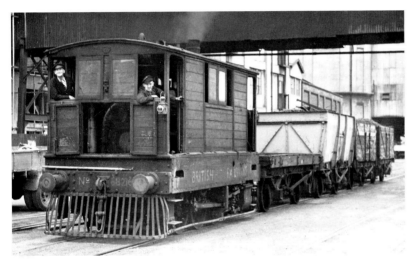

Below Road, rail and river traffic at Ipswich Docks on 27 February 1975. BR Class 03 0-6-0 diesel-mechanical shunter No 03181 survived into preservation, but the *Sophia Weston* cargo ship seen here was sunk in a collision in December 1979. *R. King*

Above Class 03 No 03179 heads a train at Ipswich Docks on 1 December 1976. Trains last used this section in 1992, although the diesel still survived in 2013. Plans to reuse the lines as a light railway link to Ipswich station were considered after closure, but track has since been removed and the route blocked by new development. *I. Cowley*

Above right The Ipswich Docks branch ran past Ipswich Lower Yard, part of which included a gas-lit cattle loading dock and an old clerestory coach, both seen here in September 1964. In 2013 disused sections of track still remained from the Upper Yard to the far side of the bridge that can be seen in the background. *Author*

Below Class 03 No 03180 crosses the River Orwell on the dock branch between Ipswich Lower and Upper yards, with a train of stone empties on 17 August 1978. Girder bridge No 249 had an axle weight restriction of 16½ tons and was responsible for the weight restriction on the branch. The tidal River Orwell changes its name to the River Gipping just upstream of the bridge, which remained disused in 2013. *J. Baker*

Above This view of part of the Lower Yard at Ipswich on 3 August 1982 includes Class 03 No 03086 shunting Freightliner stock. The line extended to the docks seen in the background. Note the National Carriers trucks, which were privatised in 1982. Disused tracks remained to the docks until 2011, when considerable sections were removed, and in 2012 the site seen here was cleared for redevelopment. *Dr L. Nixon*

Right When this view of Ranelagh Road level crossing was taken in September 2011, ex-LNER gate lamps converted to electric lighting still survived, but were not working, several years after the branch was last used. This remaining section was formally closed in March 2012. Little had changed here since the author last photographed this section of the branch in 1964, but the gates and track across the road were removed in the autumn of 2012. *Author*

10

Mystery on 'The Middy'

The history of the Mid-Suffolk Light Railway is recorded in *Lost Lines: Eastern*. Simply put, it opened in incomplete form for passengers from Haughley as far as Laxfield in 1908. What 'The Middy', as it was affectionately called, lacked in financial success was made up for in charisma, and on the last day, in July 1952, large crowds turned up to say goodbye. There were also some slightly mysterious issues associated with the railway; most can be explained – but not all.

Why at one time was the MR furtively trying to gain control of this remote, unprofitable branch? A suspicious GER discovered that the MR was contemplating extending the line, and developing it as part of a main route to an expanded port at Southwold, providing links to the continent to compete with those of the GER's port at Harwich, plans that foundered on Southwold's navigational problems.

The railway was cheaply built and station buildings were wooden-framed structures mostly covered with corrugated-iron sheets. However, at a couple of stations some metal sheets were pressed out with a brick profile and painted to try and resemble brickwork, although few were fooled.

This part of East Anglia is noted for its lack of rainfall, but oddly enough no arrangements for a sizable water tower were made at Laxfield.

Facing page At Laxfield station on 14 June 1952 the former Superintendent's office is on the right, being used as a train crew mess when this view was taken, as the line's financial administration had been transferred to Stradbroke. *R. E. Vincent*

Below The timetable for September 1948.

A temporary structure, which survived until the closure of the line, was set up involving a pumping engine that extracted water from a nearby pond. In times of drought the pond dried up, then a local stream was dammed, but the use of locomotives with limited water capacity was sometimes restricted.

Trains usually took about an hour and a half for the 19-mile trip. Passenger numbers were mostly quite limited, but official notices for many years rather curiously advised passengers that they could only book tickets at intermediate stations if there was room on the train.

The single-line method of working involved the use of a unique split staff. Each staff had two halves padlocked together; except when two trains went through the same section in the same direction. This arrangement could seem rather mystifying and, when a special officials' train ran on the line, instead of enjoying

a relaxed lunch many on board were expecting to run head on into another train at any moment.

For a time the Home signal at Kenton would not work. Staff locally knew this and trains passed it at Danger until one day a train stopped at the signal and whistled furiously. It was called on into Kenton, with surprise expressed by the station staff for this adherence to the rules. The mystery was soon solved when the Ipswich shedmaster alighted from the engine.

In one incident an engine suffered a burst boiler tube; the plugs in the tool kit just would not fit, so the crew sharpened the end of a shunter's pole and drove a piece into each end of the tube. This allowed the train to limp along, even though the end in the firebox burned off, while the smokebox door had to be left ajar to release leaking water.

In October 1964 your author arrived at Haughley with the aim of walking along the trackbed. Even at that time the course of the old line was quite difficult to

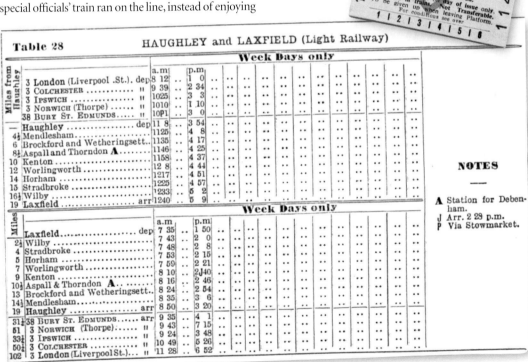

Table 28	HAUGHLEY and LAXFIELD (Light Railway)																	NOTES
		Week Days only																
Miles from Haughley		a.m	p.m	..	..	..	..	..	..	..	..	..	..	..	..	..	
3	London (Liverpool .St.). dep	8 12	1 0	..	..	..	..	..	..	..	..	..	..	..	..	..	
3	COLCHESTER .... "	9 39	2 34	..	..	..	..	..	..	..	..	..	..	..	..	..	
3	IPSWICH .... "	1025	3 3	..	..	..	..	..	..	..	..	..	..	..	..	..	
3	NORWICH (Thorpe) ...... "	1010	1 10	..	..	..	..	..	..	..	..	..	..	..	..	..	
38	BURY ST. EDMUNDS...... "	10P1	3 0	..	..	..	..	..	..	..	..	..	..	..	..	..	
—	Haughley .... dep	11 8	3 54	..	..	..	..	..	..	..	..	..	..	..	..	..	
4½	Mendlesham.................	1125	4 8	..	..	..	..	..	..	..	..	..	..	..	..	..	
6	Brockford and Wetheringsett..	1135	4 17	..	..	..	..	..	..	..	..	..	..	..	..	..	
8½	Aspall and Thorndon **A**........	1146	4 25	..	..	..	..	..	..	..	..	..	..	..	..	..	
10	Kenton....................	1158	4 37	..	..	..	..	..	..	..	..	..	..	..	..	..	**NOTES**
12	Worlingworth................	12 8	4 44	..	..	..	..	..	..	..	..	..	..	..	..	..	
14	Horham	1217	4 51	..	..	..	..	..	..	..	..	..	..	..	..	..	
15	Stradbroke	1225	4 57	..	..	..	..	..	..	..	..	..	..	..	..	..	
16½	Wilby	1233	5 2	..	..	..	..	..	..	..	..	..	..	..	..	..	**A** Station for Deben-ham.
19	Laxfield .... arr	1240	5 9	..	..	..	..	..	..	..	..	..	..	..	..	..	**J** Arr. 2 23 p.m.
		Week Days only																**P** Via Stowmarket.
Miles		a.m	p.m	..	..	..	..	..	..	..	..	..	..	..	..	..	
	Laxfield..................... dep	7 35	1 50	..	..	..	..	..	..	..	..	..	..	..	..	..	
2½	Wilby	7 43	2 0	..	..	..	..	..	..	..	..	..	..	..	..	..	
4	Stradbroke	7 48	2 8	..	..	..	..	..	..	..	..	..	..	..	..	..	
5	Horham	7 53	2 15	..	..	..	..	..	..	..	..	..	..	..	..	..	
7	Worlingworth................	7 59	2 21	..	..	..	..	..	..	..	..	..	..	..	..	..	
9	Kenton....................	8 10	2J40	..	..	..	..	..	..	..	..	..	..	..	..	..	
10½	Aspall & Thorndon **A**....	8 16	2 46	..	..	..	..	..	..	..	..	..	..	..	..	..	
13	Brockford and Wetheringsett..	8 24	2 54	..	..	..	..	..	..	..	..	..	..	..	..	..	
14½	Mendlesham.................	8 35	3 6	..	..	..	..	..	..	..	..	..	..	..	..	..	
19	Haughley .... arr	8 50	3 20	..	..	..	..	..	..	..	..	..	..	..	..	..	
31½	38 BURY ST. EDMUNDS...... arr	9 35	4 1	..	..	..	..	..	..	..	..	..	..	..	..	..	
51	3 NORWICH (Thorpe)...... "	9 43	7 15	..	..	..	..	..	..	..	..	..	..	..	..	..	
33½	3 IPSWICH .... "	9 24	3 48	..	..	..	..	..	..	..	..	..	..	..	..	..	
50½	3 COLCHESTER .... "	10 49	5 26	..	..	..	..	..	..	..	..	..	..	..	..	..	
102	3 London (Liverpool St.)... "	11 28	6 52	..	..	..	..	..	..	..	..	..	..	..	..	..	

Above On 12 July 1952 Class 'J15' 0-6-0 No 65467 is blocking the B1117 Station Road level crossing after arrival at Laxfield. Passenger services never extended beyond here. Although it is more than four years after nationalisation the advertisement boards remain headed 'London & North Eastern Railway'. *T. Rowe*

Below 'J15' 0-6-0 No 65388 stands outside the dilapidated engine shed at Laxfield – Ipswich sub-shed 32B – on 14 June 1952. The shed was so small it was said that the mice went round on their back legs. A view in *Lost Lines: Eastern* shows the shed in 1936, in rather better condition. Today a few traces of where the railway once ran may still be discovered here. *R. E. Vincent*

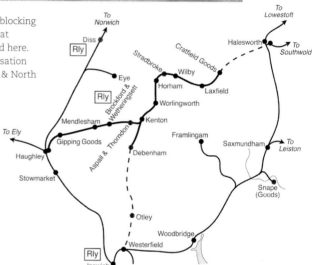

trace, as parts had already been returned to agriculture. Yet by one of the remotest of the former level crossings a mysterious voice in a broad Suffolk accent said, 'Be yer all right there, booy?' I looked around, but could see nobody in the fading light – I decided to beat a hasty return to Haughley station.

More recently I revisited the site, but it had completely vanished from the landscape. Much of the route is now obscure, but at Wetheringsett a section of line and ex-MSL buildings have been restored by the Mid-Suffolk Light Railway, a steam heritage line. Elsewhere the former Laxfield and Horham station buildings can be found at the Mangapps Farm Railway Museum.

Above right The unusual style of cast-iron lettering used at Mid-Suffolk stations, with its attractive serifs, was manufactured by Walter MacFarlane. Wilby's name board is seen here in 1952. The station was one of the smallest and most isolated on the line, consisting of a wagon body and hut. *R. E. Vincent*

Below The abandoned Laxfield station is seen circa 1953, after closure with track removed but the buildings still standing. The somewhat portable nature of the nearer timber-framed and corrugated-iron building resulted in its survival, and it was first removed to a playing field at Bedfield. In 1991 it was purchased and restored at the Mangapps Farm Railway Museum. *D. Lawrence*

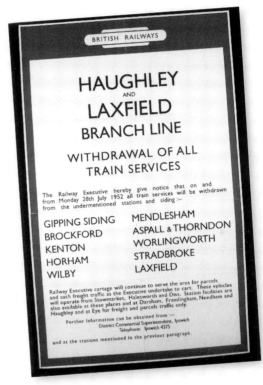

BRITISH RAILWAYS

HAUGHLEY
AND
LAXFIELD
BRANCH LINE

WITHDRAWAL OF ALL TRAIN SERVICES

The Railway Executive hereby give notice that on and from Monday 28th July 1952 all train services will be withdrawn from the undermentioned stations and siding :—

GIPPING SIDING	MENDLESHAM
BROCKFORD	ASPALL & THORNDON
KENTON	WORLINGWORTH
HORHAM	STRADBROKE
WILBY	LAXFIELD

Railway Executive cartage will continue to serve the area for parcels and such freight traffic as the Executive undertake to cart. These vehicles will operate from Stowmarket, Halesworth and Diss. Station facilities are also available at these places and at Darsham, Framlingham, Needham and Haughley and at Eye for freight and parcels traffic only.

Further information can be obtained from :—
District Commercial Superintendent, Ipswich
Telephone: Ipswich 4375

and at the stations mentioned in the previous paragraph.

11

Framlingham freight

The 5¾-mile single-line Framlingham branch ran from Wickham Market Junction on the East Suffolk line, and opened in June 1859. It served a remote agricultural area and was in many ways the quintessential English rural branch line. The river at Parham had to be diverted to accommodate the railway station, but it was a relatively lightly constructed branch. On the other hand, the intermediate station buildings on the line were of a considerable size for the settlements they served. There was both an engine and goods shed at Framlingham, and a substantial water tower.

The opening day was one of much celebration at Framlingham, with church bells ringing and speeches made – it was hailed as the town 'keeping pace with the mighty improvements of the age'. Unfortunately one of the station porters, who was also the local band master, fell in front of a train at the station, which resulted in the planned concert being cancelled.

Thereafter the line settled down to a quiet life. In 1922 Hacheston Halt was opened and conductor guards were introduced on the branch, with intermediate stations having their booking offices closed. The LNER promoted tourism to Framlingham Castle with posters and carriage prints. Summer excursions also once ran to Aldeburgh, Felixstowe and

Facing page Two coaches, converted for conductor guard working, and a freight guard's van form a Wickham Market-Framlingham mixed train on 11 October 1952. Passenger services ceased the following month. The train is seen in sylvan surroundings, between Parham and Framlingham, hauled by Class 'J15' 0-6-0 No 65467. *Ian Allan Library*

Below A weed-killing train passes Wickham Market Junction hauled by Class 'B12/3' 4-6-0 No 61533. The undated photograph was kindly given to your author by Dr Ian C. Allan when we met by chance at Ipswich station. No 61533 was withdrawn in 1959, giving a clue to the date of this view. *Dr Ian C. Allan*

Yarmouth. Freight remained important and Parham was particularly busy during the Second World War, serving the nearby airfield.

The terminus at Framlingham was located south of the town centre and passengers had to change trains at Wickham Market to reach Ipswich. Mixed trains became a feature of the line in later years, but mixing potatoes and passengers led to slow timings, and passenger numbers were low. BR closed the line to regular passenger services on 3 November 1952, after which the engine shed at Framlingham was demolished.

However, this was not the end of passenger trains on the branch, as between 1954 and 1958 Framlingham College ran special through coaches from and to London at the beginning and end of each term. The trains were available for use by the general public as well as pupils, but unfortunately it appears that some carriages were vandalised, which was used as an excuse by BR to discontinue the service. In addition, the Royal Train, including two immaculate 'B1' locomotives, was stationed overnight on the then quiet branch sidings at Marlesford in May 1956.

The opening of the MSL in 1904 had reduced the catchment area of Framlingham station, as until that time livestock had been driven to Framingham station from much of the area of mid-Suffolk served by the light railway. Livestock movement by rail on the branch had virtually ceased by the mid-1950s, but rail-served granaries at Framlingham, together with coal and sugar beet, kept the line going long after its closure to passengers. The branch was eventually worked on the 'one engine in steam' principle, with train crew operating the level crossing gates. In spite of these economies the branch was closed to freight in April 1965.

Following closure much of the line was returned to agriculture. The station buildings at Framlingham, Parham and Marlesford still exist, as do all the crossing-keepers' cottages. The coal yard at Marlesford survived for a time after the track was removed, together with the road level crossing gates, topped with their LNER oil-lit warning lamps. The branch junction station at Wickham Market on the East Suffolk line remains open.

Dr Ian C. Allan had a practice at Framlingham and there are tales of him being late for surgery when interesting workings were to be seen on the branch. He said that the town of Framlingham 'lost its heart' when the railway closed.

Left BR Sulzer Type 2 No D5045 shunts at Marlesford on 12 April 1965, a week before final closure. The diesel was one of the first of a batch of 50 engines delivered to East Anglia in 1959 to assist with the end of steam operations. After the many line closures the locomotive was transferred out of the Eastern Region in 1967 and withdrawn in 1975. *N. James*

Below D5045 is seen again waiting to leave the Framlingham branch at Wickham Market Junction with an empty coal train on the same day. Note the well-kept cuttings towards the very end of the branch's use, even after diesel workings had replaced steam. *N. James*

G. E. R.

Framlingham

Right In this closer view of the signal post, with its upper and lower arms, it can be seen that, owing to the curve and the cutting on the branch at Wickham Market Junction, the upper arm is square to the post while the lower arm is diagonal to assist visibility. The view was taken on 26 June 1966, more than a year after closure. *G. Mortimer*

MARLESFORD

Below Marlesford station survives as a private residence. Originally with eight fireplaces, the station was a substantial building for a village with a population of just a few hundred. A coach body dating from 1877, which was provided to the station as an office in 1902, was extant on the platform when this view was taken in the summer of 1970, and still survived in 2013, albeit in a more dilapidated state. The ex-GER enamel name board for Marlesford can be seen at Mangapps Railway Museum. *Author*

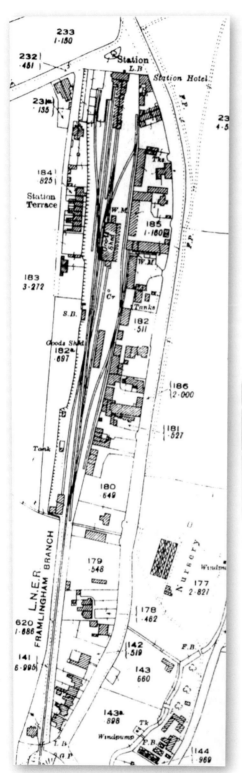

Left A map of the extensive terminus at Framlingham in 1935. *Crown Copyright*

Below To the south of Framlingham the line crossed the River Ore at Broadwater by means of a small viaduct. When this view was taken in the summer of 1990 there had been partial destruction of the solidly built structure. As much of the adjoining northern embankment had been removed, it became known locally as 'the bridge to nowhere', but survives largely unchanged in 2013. *Author*

Left The main station terminal building at Framlingham is currently used for offices and flats, while an adjoining station building survives as The Station Hotel, one of many in East Anglia. The white-brick terminal building has been externally painted but remains largely unchanged, as seen here in June 2012. An enamel name board from Framlingham can be found at Mangapps Railway Museum. *Author*

Left Framlingham station yard was once home to grain, coal and timber merchants, together with maltings, and was still being used for road freight when this view was taken in June 2012. Several of the original railway buildings remain, including this goods shed. A canopy that once protected an entrance to the goods shed had been removed since your author last visited in 1990, as part of the rebuilding of one wall of the shed. *Author*

Right On the left is the overgrown Wickham Market island platform, where connections to Ipswich could once be made from Framlingham branch trains. The goods shed is seen to the right; its railway use ended in July 1964. During the Second World War the shed was used to camouflage tanks, and the modifications to its roof to facilitate a turntable for this work were still to be seen just prior to its demolition in March 2012, when this view was taken. The unstaffed station remains open using the down platform. *Author*

12

Lost in Lowestoft

Lowestoft's growth from a small settlement to both a fishing port and a holiday destination was due to the influence of the railway. The harbour and railways were mostly developed by Samuel Peto, who was known as 'The maker of Lowestoft'. Industries were established and in many respects Lowestoft became a railway town. Even in the early 1960s about 1,000 were still in railway-related employment.

Lowestoft harbour became important for livestock and timber, but it also became the biggest fishing port of East Anglia. The GER built a new fish dock in 1865. The fish market and curing houses were originally reached by a street tramway, but in 1866 the harbour branch was extended, allowing fish to be directly loaded onto the railway.

Further railway and dock development continued and by 1900 there were almost 1,000 fishing boats using the docks, with about 55,000 tons of fish being caught that year, much being forwarded by rail to London and other major centres. Horses were used for shunting in the docks and three GER horses were among the first victims of the First World War when they were killed by bombs dropped by a German Zeppelin.

In 1960 about 18,000 tons of fish were landed, but catches were declining rapidly. In 1973 the remaining railway fish traffic ceased and today there is little left of the once mighty fishing industry. Some freight occasionally uses rail, and rusting sidings still existed west of Lowestoft station in 2013.

Facing page Class 'Y1' 0-4-0T Sentinel locomotive No 8130 is seen at the railway-served Lowestoft Borough Council Engineer's Yard on 8 August 1950. The council-owned depot was served by a siding from the main line near Coke Ovens Junction. The 'Y1s' were built by Sentinel and had a single-speed gearing, unlike the otherwise almost identical 'Y3s', which had a two-speed gear arrangement.
R. Matthews

Below A map of Lowestoft 1946. *Crown Copyright*

On the other hand, with its sandy beaches, pier and cliffside hanging gardens, Lowestoft developed an important holiday trade. The GER provided bus services and owned the South Pier; the company was once even responsible for providing brass band performances.

To the south of the tidal Lake Lothing the 1¾-mile South Side siding opened in 1859. It was originally intended as a passenger route, but the East Suffolk Railway gained access to Lowestoft Central station and it became a freight-only line. It linked to the South Quay dock areas and to a coal and goods depot at Kirkley, opening in 1904. It also served the large Co-op food factory. Kirkley depot was closed in 1966 and the last remaining section of South Side siding in November 1967.

The development of the port and the import of timber led to the establishment of Lowestoft sleeper depot, opening in 1914. The depot once employed about 60 workers on a reclaimed northern mud bank of Lake Lothing; it used imported timber

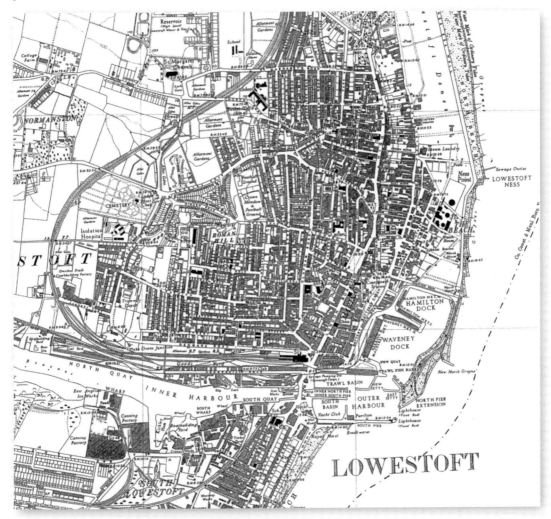

and extended to some 13 acres with a 1,000-foot (305-metre) rail-served quayside.

Internally the depot ran shunting engines and my diary reports that I visited it on 9 May 1964. Sentinel 'Y3' engines No 7 and No 40 were to be seen; it was the very last day of No 40's operation. The contraction of the railway network at that time saw the depot closed shortly after my visit.

The depot also had a 3-foot narrow-gauge system for transporting the sleepers on low trucks between the various processes of creosoting and chairing. This network used two petrol locomotives, one of which was replaced by a diesel built for the LNER in 1944; the latter still survives in private ownership.

The LNER also opened a precast concrete sleeper depot on the site of the old saw mill, employing at its peak about 100 workers. The depot eventually served the whole of BR Eastern Region, and two or three trains departed from the depot each week. The concrete sleeper section closed in 1985 and the remaining sidings to the site in 1988. The area has subsequently been redeveloped.

The last railway to open in Lowestoft was the NSJ coastal link to Yarmouth South Town, with services commencing in July 1903. The line provided the suburban Lowestoft North station. After closure of the Beccles-Yarmouth South Town direct line trains were diverted via Lowestoft and the ex-NSJ line to Yarmouth. Freight ceased in November 1967, but

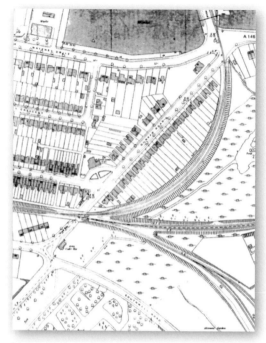

Above A three-way junction on the South Side Siding in 1945. The top line ran to the Co-operative food factory, the middle line to Belvedere Road goods and the bottom line to Kirkley goods. *Crown Copyright*

passenger closure was keenly contested and it was the last major line and station to close at Lowestoft, in May 1970. The Lowestoft North station site is now occupied by a residential area, aptly named Beeching Drive.

Right The 'Y1' is seen again shunting at Lowestoft harbour on 17 March 1953. Note the close proximity of shops and flats to the rail lines, although cow-catchers were not required as the dock rail lines were mostly separated from the roads. The engine, which looks to be in good external condition, was built in 1925 and survived, renumbered as Departmental No 37, until 1956. *R. E. Vincent*

Above A renumbering of the shunting engines into departmental allocations was undertaken in 1953, and Class 'Y3' 0-4-0T Departmental No 38 was photographed at Lowestoft on 20 April 1954. The engine was allocated to Lowestoft between 1950 and 1959. Work involved shunting and hauling trains to and from the harbour, which was once very busy with rail traffic, particularly fish. Note the sand boxes to both wheels. *R. E. Vincent*

Right Class 'Y3' 0-4-0T Departmental No 41 stands at Lowestoft sleeper depot on 28 May 1960. The author was privileged to ride in the cab of sister engine No 40 on its last day of operation on Saturday 9 May 1964. The ride was noted as being rough, steam-filled and slow, and it was also noted that the engine was being fuelled by wood. *Ian Allan Library*

Right This is the exterior of Lowestoft North station in 1969. The station was located close to the sea and once had a BR camping coach. Booking staff were withdrawn in 1966 and it became an unstaffed halt. It was closed to remaining freight in November 1967 and to passengers in May 1970. The buildings were demolished after closure, but the nearby station house remains. *Author*

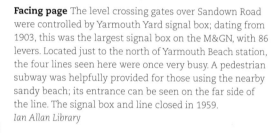

Below Part of the most easterly closed track in the British Isles: this section of Lowestoft harbour line, by the Trawl Basin, is seen in March 2012, some 40 years after it was last used. The track is liberally interspersed with gullies that also allowed run-off from the sunken rail grooves. Loaded fish trains were sometimes held here and the melting water from the ice used for refrigeration could have caused a wet quayside. *Author*

Facing page The level crossing gates over Sandown Road were controlled by Yarmouth Yard signal box; dating from 1903, this was the largest signal box on the M&GN, with 86 levers. Located just to the north of Yarmouth Beach station, the four lines seen here were once very busy. A pedestrian subway was helpfully provided for those using the nearby sandy beach; its entrance can be seen on the far side of the line. The signal box and line closed in 1959. *Ian Allan Library*

Below A train departs from Lowestoft North in the winter of 1969. The well-used Lowestoft-Yarmouth route served a number of coastal holiday camps, but was singled in 1962; the stations were left unmodernised and unstaffed and for the most part became derelict and vandalised. *Author*

13

Gone from Great Yarmouth

Great Yarmouth, with its sandy beaches, was transformed by the railways from a small settlement to a major seaside resort. The town also had an important fishing fleet; once consisting of more than 1,000 boats, it has now gone, together with many of the railways, but Yarmouth remains an important holiday destination. There were once four lines to the town, but today there is just one, and one station, Yarmouth Vauxhall, which was the first to open in 1844.

The M&GN line to Yarmouth Beach station opened in August 1877 and was well-sited, being, as its name suggests, close to the beach. A new halt was added on this line by the LNER at Newtown, on the northern outskirts of Yarmouth, in 1933. Immediately after the Second World War summer passenger traffic was still intense, and even in the 1950s peak summer holiday trains ran to and from many parts of England.

Yet in the winter there was surplus capacity and travel patterns were changing rapidly, with greater car and coach usage and more holidays being taken abroad. The ex-M&GN line to Yarmouth Beach was considered by BR to duplicate the ex-GER route to the town and was the first line and station to close, in February 1959. Following closure the Beach station buildings remained until 1986, being used by the bus station that had taken over the site. Today preserved short sections of track and two original cast iron supports are to be found on the site of the station, which is now a car park.

A dockside freight tramway, first authorised for horse traction in 1845, together with other later tram lines, connected Yarmouth Vauxhall and Beach stations to the North, Hall and South quays on the River Yare. The tramway enabled fish, herring in particular, to be transported directly by rail from the quayside. It was worked for many years by three steam tram engines, before the first diesel took over in 1952. White Swan coal yard closed in 1970, but the final section of tramway was not officially closed until the end of 1975.

The 12½-mile GER direct Yarmouth South Town-Beccles line had opened throughout by June 1859. The route involved two swing bridges over the River Waveney at St Olaves and north of Beccles. Both bridges had very low speed restrictions and until 1927 strict rules required there to be pilotmen in the cabs of trains crossing the bridges. Although peak holiday traffic using this section of the main

Below A map of Great Yarmouth in 1958. *Crown Copyright*

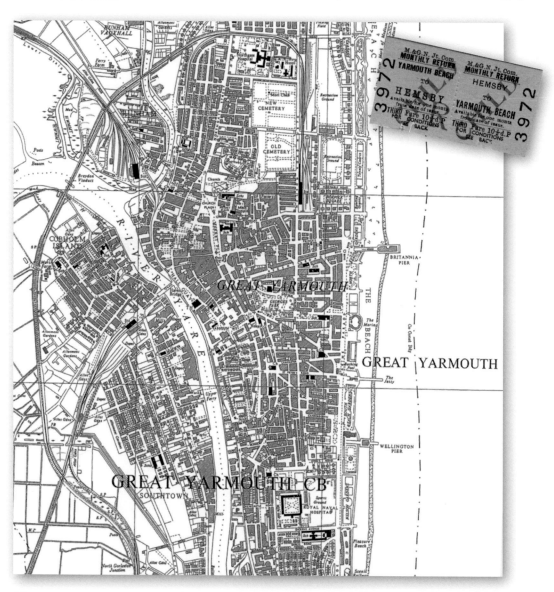

line to and from London was extensive, because of the swing bridges the line was costly to maintain and closed in November 1959, with trains being diverted through Lowestoft and the ex-NSJ line, via Gorleston-on-Sea. The closure gave the latter resorts a better service and in general the direct line was not greatly missed.

The 11-mile NSJ Lowestoft-Yarmouth South Town route opened in 1903. It was a modern railway with electrically lit platforms and just one level crossing. A short line linked the NSJ to the M&GN and was carried over Breydon Water by an 800-foot (243-metre) steel viaduct of four fixed spans and a double opening span. This link was the first passenger line to close in the Yarmouth area, being

Below Drewry diesel No 11101 runs along Yarmouth Hall Quay, near the imposing Town Hall, on 15 July 1952. The locomotive had been delivered to Yarmouth as new in June of that year and was withdrawn in 1968. Prior to the Second World War the quayside was immensely busy, particularly with freight associated with the fleet of coal-fired steam fishing trawlers. *B. Lockey*

taken out of use in 1953, although demolition of the viaduct did not begin until 1962.

Yarmouth South Town station had an attractive classical Italianate frontage and train shed. The terminus was modernised by BR with new platform canopies, booking hall, refreshment room and signal box. In the Beeching Report it was classified with passenger revenues on a par with Norwich, Cambridge and Ipswich, but was allowed to become a derelict and unstaffed halt.

The very controversial and late closure of this line came in May 1970, severing the important Yarmouth-Lowestoft coastal route and leaving Gorleston-on-Sea without a train service. The line also served many holiday camps and resorts between Yarmouth and Lowestoft, but stations had been allowed to become derelict and vandalised, and all through services were withdrawn. Yarmouth South Town and Gorleston stations have since been demolished and the large former railway areas redeveloped, including part of the route north of Gorleston being turned into a road.

Left Here is a closer view of No 11101 on Yarmouth quay, by Fishers Quay, in the 1950s. Note the busy quayside road scene with a BR three-wheeled Scammell tractor unit and an Aveling & Barford diesel road-roller. The buildings nearest the engine have since been demolished. *D. Lawrence*

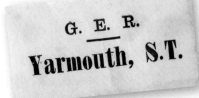

G. E. R.

Yarmouth, S.T.

Right Vauxhall Bridge, No 1277 over the River Bure outside Yarmouth Vauxhall station, is a listed structure dating from 1848. The three lattice bowstring arches were added to the original box girder bridge in 1886 to increase its load-carrying capacity prior to the introduction of steam tram engines. This view was taken in March 2012, when a short section of steeply graded tramway track nearby leading to the bridge could still be found. *Author*

Below Class 'F4' 2-4-2T No 67154 stands at Yarmouth South Town shed on 20 June 1951, a few months before its withdrawal. Yarmouth's railway importance is reflected by the fact that the town once had three engine sheds, South Town (32D), Vauxhall (32E) and Beach (32F); all closed in 1959. South Town shed had 22 engines in 1950; it was rebuilt in 1956, but housed just six locomotives at the time of its closure to steam. The building evaded demolition until 1979. *E. Patterson*

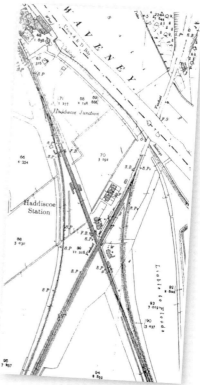

Above Haddiscoe High Level signal box survives and is seen in March 2012. The substantial brick signal box was built on concrete pier legs to ensure that flooding would not cause operating difficulties. The box had a commanding view of the railway as well as the River Waveney and controlled the adjoining Haddiscoe swing bridge, which was sometimes known as the St Olaves swing bridge. *Author*

Right Haddiscoe stations, showing the former connecting lines and the location of the swing bridge in 1960. *Crown Copyright*

Below The substantial blue engineering brick supports of Haddiscoe swing bridge were photographed in March 2012. The circular foundation nearest the camera was the base of the new electrically controlled swing bridge installed by the LNER in 1926. The metal portions of the bridge were dismantled for scrap after its closure in November 1959. *Author*

Above The 11.10am Lowestoft Central-Yarmouth South Town DMU moves away from Hopton-on-Sea station on 29 April 1970, the final week of service on the ex-NSJ line. The station once had a BR camping coach; all is now demolished and the area redeveloped. *G. Mortimer*

Below A DMU calls at Corton-on-Sea with a Lowestoft Central-Yarmouth South Town service during the summer of 1969. The station once had a BR camping coach. The line's platelayer can be seen on the track – he walked the single line once a week at this time. Note that the canopy was retained only on the platform that was not in use! The station building is the only one on the ex-NSJ line to survive today. *P. Groom*

Facing page Getting the right station for your luggage could sometimes be tricky. Felixstowe station seen here opened in 1877, but was called Beach after the opening of the Town station in 1898. Beach station remained open for summer services until September 1967. All the platform buildings seen here were demolished in 1994, but freight still uses the track towards Felixstowe Pier station, which closed in 1951 and is now lost within Felixstowe Dock. Felixstowe Dock was also to be found in the timetable, where a railway ferry ran to Harwich Pier. *Author*

14

Lost luggage

Sending luggage in advance, or travelling with luggage, developed as a well-known feature of the railways. Luggage barrows pushed by porters and piled high with wooden trunks and leather cases, adorned with railway luggage labels, could once be seen at many stations. The Victorians did not travel light, and in 1848 the Eastern Counties Railway lost around 80 items of luggage in a single day. This highlighted the need for clear labelling.

Eventually, and usually once a ticket had been purchased, the railway could collect your luggage from your home and deliver it to your destination address, within specified limits. For a smaller fee passengers could carry their own luggage to and from the nearest stations concerned. Even if you were travelling with your luggage, a label was often required and most trains provided luggage vans.

GER luggage labels date from 1862 and simply provided the destination, but from about 1900 the standard GER label also had a blank space to indicate the origin of the luggage. This 'From' line was filled in by pencil or the station stamp, or some major stations had them pre-printed. GER labels were printed at the railway's own works at Stratford.

Luggage label storage racks were once found at almost all East Anglian stations. The racks were stocked with a large range of the labels to the most popular destinations from the station concerned. The labels were organised in pigeonholes, in alphabetical order, and a pot of glue to affix them was usually found nearby.

The GER provided labels for almost every station in East Anglia. Route labels for longer distances beyond East Anglia, such as on the GN&GE line, were also provided in distinctive colours and with route symbols. Elsewhere in East Anglia the Southwold Railway provided its own luggage labels, as did the M&GN, NSJ and CVH.

When the LNER took over it first changed the label heading, but went on to produce smaller luggage and routing labels. In a sensible cost-saving exercise, these were often only issued when the stocks of pre-Grouping labels were exhausted, while variants to the standard issues of labels could be found.

The BR luggage label was introduced when the railways were nationalised in 1948. It was a single label, with space to write the name of the station from which the luggage was being dispatched and that to which it was destined, via which route and region. Even so, pre-Grouping labels could still be found at most stations into the mid-1960s.

The use of labels gradually diminished with the decreasing use of the railways for holidays, particularly after the Second World War, and the closure of stations. The golden age of luggage proudly covered with railway labels was lost. Eventually luggage could generally only be accepted by the railways if it was lugged along by passengers themselves – but lost luggage offices still survive.

Above Luggage could be sent in advance to the luxurious railway-owned Felix Hotel, via Felixstowe Town station. The hotel opened in 1903 and Wallis Simpson was among its guests. It closed in 1952, but still survives in residential use, and much of the impressive cliff-top building is unchanged. Part of the Palm Court is seen here in April 2013. *Author's collection*

Left Aldeburgh station's train shed, seen here in the early 1950s, would have kept your luggage dry. In later years the accumulation of soot and grime on the glass section of roof made the interior quite dark and gas lights within it burned much of the time. Outside the delightful station gardens won many prizes. The train shed was demolished in August 1965, before closure of the branch in September 1966. All remaining buildings were demolished in 1975 and housing built on the site. *D. Raynesford*

Right Two series of six postcards were produced by Reg Carter, called 'The Sorrows of Southwold', lampooning the Southwold Railway. The contents of some luggage on Southwold's station platform are to be noted! The postcards were originally sold in brown paper envelopes. *Author's collection*

Left The Southwold Railway closed in 1929 and was the first important loss in East Anglia. After closure, Southwold station remained in a forlorn and ever-increasingly derelict state, as seen here, until it was demolished in 1964. The luggage van, just visible against the far wall, survived into preservation. Luggage labels to Southwold were still to be found in the 1960s, well over 30 years after closure, as arrangements for the alternative road transport of luggage were made by the LNER. *Author's collection*

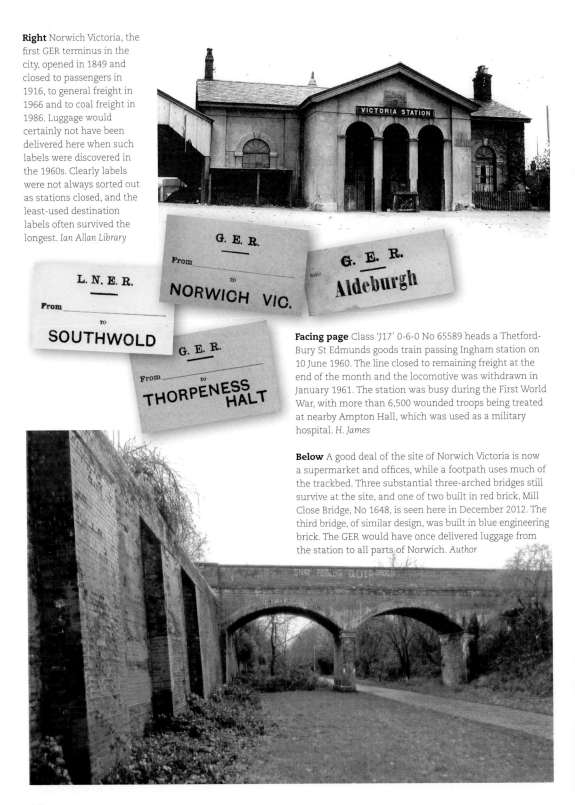

Right Norwich Victoria, the first GER terminus in the city, opened in 1849 and closed to passengers in 1916, to general freight in 1966 and to coal freight in 1986. Luggage would certainly not have been delivered here when such labels were discovered in the 1960s. Clearly labels were not always sorted out as stations closed, and the least-used destination labels often survived the longest. *Ian Allan Library*

Facing page Class 'J17' 0-6-0 No 65589 heads a Thetford-Bury St Edmunds goods train passing Ingham station on 10 June 1960. The line closed to remaining freight at the end of the month and the locomotive was withdrawn in January 1961. The station was busy during the First World War, with more than 6,500 wounded troops being treated at nearby Ampton Hall, which was used as a military hospital. *H. James*

Below A good deal of the site of Norwich Victoria is now a supermarket and offices, while a footpath uses much of the trackbed. Three substantial three-arched bridges still survive at the site, and one of two built in red brick, Mill Close Bridge, No 1648, is seen here in December 2012. The third bridge, of similar design, was built in blue engineering brick. The GER would have once delivered luggage from the station to all parts of Norwich. *Author*

15

Bury branches

Bury St Edmunds was once the focal point of four lines. The routes helped local industries such as milling and brewing to grow, while a large sugar beet factory was established in 1925. The main granaries, maltings and sugar beet factory were rail-connected and substantial rail freight was once handled in the area. The lines to Ipswich and Ely remain, but those to Thetford and Long Melford are closed.

The link from Thetford started with an east-facing spur from the Cambridge-Norwich line running south to Thetford Bridge station, opened by the Thetford & Watton Railway in November 1875; this avoided the need for trains from Watton and Swaffham to reverse into this station via the west-facing spur. The railway also ran the 12¾-mile Thetford Bridge-Bury line, which opened in March of the following year. The prospect of a rival independent route through the centre of East Anglia resulted in the GER taking over these lines in 1878.

After this date trains ran directly into Thetford's GER main-line station and the east curve to Thetford Bridge was closed.

As it turned out the Bury-Thetford branch remained a rural backwater and was never particularly busy, except during the two World Wars. During the Great War a military depot was opened at Little Heath near Barnham station, which included the storage of mustard gas to combat deadly German gases. During the Second World War it was used as a key munitions store serving the RAF Bomber Command. Sidings

Table 40	BURY ST. EDMUNDS and THETFORD											Week Days only		
Miles		**Week Days only**				**Miles**		a.m		a.m	p.m p.m	
		a.m	a.m	a m	p.m			a.m		a.m	p.m p.m	
38	London(L'pool St) dep	..	5 50	1025	1 0	1	Thetford .... dep	8 35	..	1135	3 15 6 35	..
—	Bury St. Edmunds..dep	7 2	1040	1 40	4 23	1	Thetford Bridge	8 39	..	1139	3 19 6 39	..
3¾	Ingham...............	7 11	1049	1 49	4 32	3¾	Barnham...............	8 45	..	1145	3 25 6 45	..
5½	Seven Hills Halt........	7 16	1054	1 54	4 39	7	Seven Hills Halt........	8 52	..	1152	3 32 6 52	..
9¼	Barnham...............	7 22	11 0	2 0	4 45	9	Ingham...............	8 57	..	1157	3 37 6 57	..
11¼	Thetford Bridge	7 28	11 6	2 6	4 51	12½	Bury St. Edmunds. arr	9 5	..	12 5	3 45 7 5	..
12½	Thetford .... arr	7 33	1112	2 11	4 58	98	38 London(L'pool St) arr	12 K 7	..	3 37	6 52, 11 A 19	..

A Via Cambridge.   K Via Long Melford and Mark's Tey.

Tickets from Seven Hills Halt, Barnham, and Thetford Bridge are issued on train.
Passengers to or from Seven Hills Halt must travel in special car provided.

Above The timetable for September 1948.

were provided and generated considerable freight on the line, while locomotives using the sidings were fitted with spark arrestors. Even after the war decommissioning of the site provided additional freight for the branch until 1955.

The line closed to passengers in June 1953, when 'The Thetford Flyer', as it was known locally, made its last trip bedecked with a wreath. The line closed to remaining freight in June 1960. The attractive station buildings at Barnham and Thetford Bridge, in knapped (split) flint, have been demolished, but the trackbed is visible in many areas, including the siding to Little Heath, together with Ingham station.

The 16½-mile Bury St Edmunds-Long Melford route opened in August 1865. The single line served Lavenham, an agricultural market and textile town, but the area continued to decline. The line was always somewhat of a secondary route, even though

some services ran from Bury St Edmunds through to Marks Tey and Colchester, and occasional excursions used the line to and from London or Clacton. Nevertheless, local passenger traffic was always light, and the Bury-Ipswich-Colchester line duplicated the route for long-distance services.

The station at Bury East Gate closed to passenger services as early as May 1909, although it was used in 1914 for a nearby agricultural show. DMUs were introduced in 1959, replacing elderly rolling stock, but they could not reverse the line's decline and passenger services ended in April 1961. Freight between Bury and Lavenham lasted until April 1965. The station buildings at Bury East Gate and Lavenham have been demolished, and Cockfield station platform building remains in a derelict condition, but Welnetham, after a period of dereliction, survives in residential use.

Left The two-coach 1.44pm Bury St Edmunds-Thetford train leaves Bury hauled by Class 'F6' 2-4-2T No 67236 on 25 April 1953. The train was sometimes locally known as 'The Thetford Flyer'. Speed on the curve was limited to 15mph, but 45mph was more normal elsewhere on the single-line branch. Conductor guards had been introduced in October 1922. *G. Mortimer*

Right A map of Lavenham in 1958. *Crown Copyright*

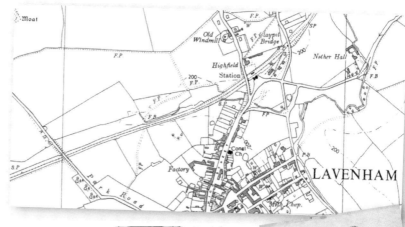

Below The only station building to survive on the Bury St Edmunds-Thetford branch is Ingham, seen here in March 2012. Situated in one of the deepest cuttings on the branch, the knapped-flint passenger building and station house was of similar design to others on the line. *Author*

Below This undated view of Barnham station, with its knapped-flint station master's house, was probably taken soon after the track was lifted in 1963. The village sign still shows a railway station, there is still a Station Road, and most of the buildings seen here remained for some time after closure, before being demolished. *A. Muckley*

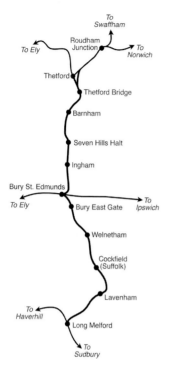

Right This cast-iron open-air urinal, rusting on the overgrown platform, survived at Cockfield in January 1982. It was curious in that most East Anglian stations that provided toilet facilities did so within the main building. The faded green-painted structure was later preserved at the East Anglian Railway Museum at Chappel & Wakes Colne. *Author*

Right An arched red-brick railway bridge is being demolished near Cockfield in January 1982. Although parts of the line have been obliterated and returned to agriculture, many remains, including bridges, are still to be found along the branch. *Author*

Below The single-platform Cockfield station was renamed Cockfield Suffolk in 1927 to distinguish it from the station of the same name in County Durham; it closed to passengers in April 1961 and to remaining freight four years later. The passenger station building remained abandoned in June 2012, when this view was taken, with little significant change since its closure. *Author*

16

Class 'J15' 0-6-0 No 65438 runs round its train at the Mildenhall terminus on 25 January 1958. Land was purchased for the line to become double track, but plans to extend the railway over the River Lark beyond the buffers in the distance never materialised, and the branch always remained a single line. *Ian Allan Library*

Four ways from Fordham

In 1964 my father was persuaded to take a detour near Cambridge and drive to a derelict station called Quy. Scattered amongst the closed remains were an old oil lamp that was too rusty to salvage and some wagon labels that had once been used on wagons to the station – such was the state of many derelict stations in the 1960s. So what line had we stumbled across? It was the 19-mile Barnwell-Fordham-Mildenhall branch.

In short, after considerable difficulty in raising capital the Barnwell-Fordham section opened in 1884 and the Fordham-Mildenhall section the following year. Original plans were for the line to continue on to Thetford and Norwich, but the route never extended beyond Mildenhall and the branch remained a single line.

The section that was built was intended to help the depressed agricultural economy of the area and agricultural freight became important, together with imported coal to the local settlements on the branch. Yet it was a sparsely populated area, several stations were not well sited for the settlements they served, and passenger economies were considered early on. A hand-operated turntable was provided at Mildenhall, but push-pull working was introduced in 1913. This form of working proved unsatisfactory on busy market days and conventional trains were soon reinstated on the branch. Old coaches were converted with a centre gangway and corridors to enable the conductor guard to issue tickets on the train for Quy and the halts.

The three rather primitive halts on the line had no raised platforms, being little more than a sign and an oil lamp. Worlington Golf Links Halt was provided exclusively for the adjoining golf club. Retractable steps controlled from the guard's van were used by passengers to board and leave the train at the halts.

In 1923 the LNER took over the line, but little changed. Seaside and London excursion trains from the branch stations were run and were usually well patronised. Mildenhall RAF air base was opened in 1934, then in 1936 the first air show was held and spectators began to use the railway. During the Second World War the line was busy with airmen and freight destined for the airfield, which became one of the largest bomber air bases in the country.

The elderly rolling stock was replaced by lightweight diesel railcars, introduced by BR in 1958. The branch cut across the main Ely-Ipswich line at Fordham, and some Mildenhall-Cambridge trains were run via Newmarket and to Ely, but without huge success. A competing bus service to USAF Mildenhall was provided from Shippea Hill. The line remained a relatively quiet rural branch and closed to passengers in June 1962. Freight services ceased in July 1964, apart from the Fordham-Burwell section, which closed in April 1965, and a short section to an oil

depot at Barnwell Junction, whose disused tracks still remained in 2013.

My diary records that in April 1965 the Fordham-Mildenhall section had already been lifted. Fordham station remained open until September 1965 and the buildings survived in a derelict state, as did those at Bottisham & Lode, in 2013. Most other branch stations have been restored for residential use. The station building at Quy is in commercial use and the trackbed here has become a farm track. Elsewhere much of the trackbed has been returned to agriculture. At Fordham, freight trains still rumble past the derelict station on the Ely-Ipswich line.

Below The Mildenhall branch timetable for 1948.

Table 39	CAMBRIDGE and MILDENHALL										
	Week Days only					Miles		**Week Days only**			
Miles		a.m	a.m	p.m	p.m			a.m	a.m	p.m	p.m
	4 London(L'poolSt.)dep	4 20	8 20	2 25	5J54	1	Mildenhall ....dep	7 42	11 50	5 48	9 0
12	" (King'sC.) "		8 12	2 0	..	1	Worlington Golf Links	7 46	11 54	5 52	..
—	Cambridge.........dep	6 33	1028	4 27	7 45	4	Isleham ....[Halt	7 53	12 1	5 59	9 9
1¼	Barnwell	6 37	1032	4 31	7 49	7½	Fordham.........{arr	7 59	12 7	6 6	9 15
2½	Fen Ditton Halt........	..	1035	4 34	7 52		{ dep	8 6	12 9	6 7	9 16
4½	Quy	6 45	1041	4 40	7 58	10	Exning Road Halt......	8 13	12 16	6 15	..
6	Bottisham and Lode....	6 51	1045	4 44	8 2	10½	Burwell	8 16	12 19	6 18	..
8	Swaffhamprior.........	6 56	1050	4 49	8 7	12½	Swaffhamprior.........	8 20	12 23	6 22	..
10	Burwell	7 3	1055	4 54	8 12	14½	Bottisham and Lode....	8 26	12 28	6 27	..
10½	Exning Road Halt......	..	1058	4 57	8 15	16½	Quy	8 30	12 32	6 31	..
13½	Fordham.........{ arr	7 11	11 5	5 4	8 22	18½	Fen Ditton Halt........	8 35	12 37	6 36	..
	{ dep	7 14	1110	5 10	8 24	19	Barnwell	8 38	12 40	6 39	..
16¾	Isleham ....[Halt..	7 22	1117	5 17	8 31	20½	Cambridge.........arr	8 47	12 45	6 43	9 52
19¼	Wor'ington Golf Links	..	1124	5 24	8 38	78½	12 London(King'sC.) arr	11 0	..	..	..
20¾	Mildenhall ....arr	7 31	1127	5 27	8 41	76¼	4 " (L'poolSt.) "	10 30	2 40	8 45	2a30

a a.m J 3 mins. later on Fridays until 29th October inclusive

Tickets from Quy and the Halts are issued on train.
Passengers to or from the Halts must travel in special car provided

Below Class 'E4' 2-4-0 No 62785 leaves Fordham with the
6.28am Cambridge-Mildenhall mixed train on 1 May 1958.
The locomotive was one of the last 2-4-0s to survive in
Britain and was subsequently preserved as part of the
National Collection. It is currently to be found at
Bressingham. *P. Wells*

Little and large at Fordham: Class 'B17' 4-6-0 No 61645
The Suffolk Regiment, with a train from Peterborough to
Cambridge via Newmarket, stands next to a four-wheel
48-seat lightweight German-built diesel railbus. The latter
was on trial on the Mildenhall branch, with a view to effect
economies, when this view was taken in May 1958.
D. Penney

Left The well-preserved wooden station buildings at Quy are seen in March 2012, some 50 years after closure to passengers, and now in use by small businesses. The brick-built station house also survives here. The station was located some considerable way from the village it served, indicating the significance of agricultural rather than passenger traffic at this location, although freight survived for only two years after closure to passengers. *Author*

Below Ivatt Class 2 2-6-0 No 46467 brings the Mildenhall branch freight into Barnwell Junction station near Cambridge on 20 April 1960. The locomotive had been delivered new to Cambridge in 1951, but was transferred to Scotland in 1961, due to the early dieselisation of East Anglian lines. *G. King*

Above The 1879 Fordham station building predated the other branch stations and was built mainly with white bricks. The distinctive design is seen here in March 2012. The disused station house, which continued to be occupied after the station closed in September 1965, had been abandoned since the author last visited in 1994. *Author*

Below The derelict station buildings at Bottisham & Lode are seen here in March 2012. Lode was added to the station's name in 1897. The red-brick buildings and station master's house were accompanied by nearby porter's housing. The station design is very similar to that at Mildenhall.
Author's collection

17

Going to St Ives

St Ives grew as a market town on the River Ouse, but with the arrival of the railways became a focus for no fewer than four routes. Agricultural freight developed on all the lines, but passenger flows were greatest on the St Ives-Cambridge line, and until the late 1950s St Ives was a busy railway junction.

The 14¾-mile Cambridge-St Ives line opened in August 1847. Part of the first railway to open to St Ives, it was the last to be closed to regular passengers in October 1970. Sand freight remained on the Cambridge-Fen Drayton section until 1992, but by this time had been reduced to one train a week. A number of special passenger excursion trains also continued to run and there was much lobbying for the line to be reopened to passengers. After formal closure in August 2003, there was a fierce debate as to its future use and, following considerable delay, much of the former railway line is now used as a guided busway, which opened in August 2011.

The 19-mile St Ives-March line opened in 1848, originally as part of a longer link to Wisbech. In 1879 most of the line became the southern part of the GN&GE strategic route to the north. The line from Cambridge to March via St Ives also provided a useful diversionary route for coal trains around a once congested Ely and was known locally as 'The St Ives

Loop Line'. The St Ives-March line closed to passengers in March 1967, having closed to freight a year earlier.

The GN&GE also extended 5¼ miles from St Ives to Huntingdon. This section had originally also opened in 1847, but was cheaply constructed and was notorious for its weak bridges over the River Ouse and its backwaters, some with a 10mph speed restriction and all with weight restrictions. As a consequence its potential as a long-distance route was reduced, although Kettering-Cambridge passenger trains used the line. The single line closed to its remaining Fridays-only passenger train in September 1959, although freight remained on a western Huntingdon-Godmanchester stub until June 1962.

The first section of the Ely-St Ives line opened as far as Sutton in April 1865, being completed through to Needingworth Junction and thence to St Ives in May 1878. Many stations on the 17¾-mile route were not well located for the settlements they served. In 1922 the GER withdrew the booking office staff from all the intermediate stations except Haddenham; however, these economies were not enough to save the passenger service and, as the last route to be opened to St Ives, it was the first to close to regular passenger services in February 1931.

Above Class 31 No 5694 in green livery runs round a sand train at St Ives during the summer of 1971. An aggregate company was active in extracting sand in this area, and seepage of sand from some wagons resulted in a sandy trail on sections of the track. *I. Hodson*

Special summer passenger trains of fruit-pickers continued to use the line and excursions to Hunstanton in particular were run until 1958, when the Bluntisham-Sutton part of the line closed. Freight survived on the two short end sections of the route until October 1964, while part of the line between Earith Bridge and Sutton was used as a wagon store. Remaining track was lifted in 1965, but remains of the trackbed are still to be found at Sutton and elsewhere on the route. Today St Ives, once so well served by railways, has none.

Left A trainload of concrete beams is ready for departure from St Ives on 30 November 1961, headed by Class 'B1' 4-6-0 No 61005 *Bongo*. The train was bound for the Watford area in connection with a new road bridge over the railway. The locomotive, based at March shed, was withdrawn the following year. *BR*

Left The 16.04 Cambridge-St Ives train is seen at Swavesey on 2 October 1970, during the final week of regular passenger trains on the branch. The passengers walking in front of the DMU are local schoolchildren. The station was demolished in 2007 to make way for a guided busway. *G. Mortimer*

Below Class 31 No 5634 shunts wagons at St Ives station, ready to form a sand freight train back to Cambridge in May 1971. The St Ives-Fen Drayton section was closed in 1976, with a road being built over part of this trackbed to serve a rail freight terminal at Fen Drayton. From here the aggregates were transported over the remaining branch until this rail traffic ceased in 1992. *I. Hodson*

Right St Ives departing 1933.

Above Seen from Histon level crossing, a special train waits to depart for Swavesey. Histon station remains remarkably intact almost a decade after regular passenger services were withdrawn. The jam factory at Histon was located close to the railway and seasonal fruit was delivered by rail until 1983. *B. Philpot*

Below The disused platforms and track seen in *Lost Lines: Eastern* have been removed at Histon in favour of a guided busway. The main station building remains, after much protest against its demolition, although was unused when this view was taken in March 2012. Trains from Cambridge station to Histon took less than 10 minutes – the guided bus takes almost half an hour. *Author*

Below right The last post at Somersham: the main wooden passenger station building was removed and rebuilt at Sir William McAlpine's private museum at Fawley near Henley-on-Thames. Nevertheless, a concrete level crossing gate post was still to be found on the ex-GN&GE line at Somersham station when this view was taken in August 2008. *Author*

18

Swaffham by gaslight

In 1848 the 26½-mile King's Lynn-Dereham line, via Swaffham, opened throughout, with an original plan to extend to Yarmouth. Almost midway between King's Lynn and Dereham, Swaffham became a junction for Watton and Thetford in 1875. The Wymondham-Dereham section had opened the previous year, and this enabled a Great Yarmouth-King's Lynn route to be established via Swaffham. As a consequence, the GER ran some semi-fast trains over the line, competing with the M&GN route via Melton Constable.

Fertile agricultural land adjoined much of the railway and the line developed significant agriculture traffic. In the 1920s sugar beet traffic built up and the LNER did much to encourage local farmers to use the railway to convey their crop to the factory at South Lynn and, at busy times, to Wissington.

The LNER also promoted tourism to Castle Acre near Swaffham, and rationalised the signalling at the station, closing two existing signal boxes and opening a new one in 1925. There was considerable troop activity at Swaffham during the Second World War, and the railway station became one of the few bomb-damaged buildings in the town.

The King's Lynn-Swaffham-Wymondham line was not proposed for closure in the Beeching Report, but was recommended to remain as a route for express

Facing page A DMU destined for King's Lynn draws into Wendling on 22 June 1963. During the Second World War the station was busy with military personnel to and from the nearby airbase. After closure in 1968 the station, with all its railway trappings seen here, was used for filming scenes in *Dad's Army*, but was demolished in the early 1970s and a road now runs through the site. *J. Spencer Gilks*

Below A Brush Type 2 is seen at Swaffham on 13 June 1963. The goods yard closed in 1966 and the track was removed, with just a passing loop remaining operational after that date. All the freight-related buildings seen in this view have survived in industrial and storage use. *Author*

freight and passenger trains, but with intermediate stations, other than Swaffham and Dereham, being closed. DMUs had been introduced in 1955, signalling and track was simplified, and in August 1966 all stations became unstaffed halts.

There was little other improvement; road crossings and signalling were not automated and long-term investment was not forthcoming. A Norwich-King's Lynn rail alternative, of sorts, existed via Ely, most trains continued to stop at all stations, and passenger closure came in September 1968. Freight on the Wymondham-Dereham section survived until June 1989, and the King's Lynn-Middleton Towers section still remains open for sand trains.

There is an interesting entry in my diary for 4 March 1967: 'The Norwich-King's Lynn, via Dereham, route was now a single line. The driver let me into his cab [can you imagine that now!] and we discussed closures. He had once fired "B1s" around the Clacton area and had criticisms of the railway management.' It is also clear from my diary that some trains over the Swaffham-Thetford branch were primarily for schoolchildren and did not run during the school holidays, resulting in a long wait on the day of my visit during Easter!

Today several of the former station buildings remain, mainly in residential use. Parts of the Middleton Towers-Dereham trackbed are used as local tracks, a road and even a fish lake. At Dereham the railway has been reopened as part of the Mid-Norfolk Railway, a heritage line. The line runs south to Wymondham and the aim is to run north on the Wells branch to County School and even Fakenham. This will make it one of the longest preserved lines in the country, and will return a railway to an area that lost its trains in the 1960s. However, trains are unlikely to return to Swaffham.

Right The fact that Swaffham's station platforms were still gas-lit in 1968, when this view was taken, demonstrates the long-term lack of investment in parts of the rural railway infrastructure at that time. Electric lighting had even been installed at Southwold station in 1905. *J. Vaughan*

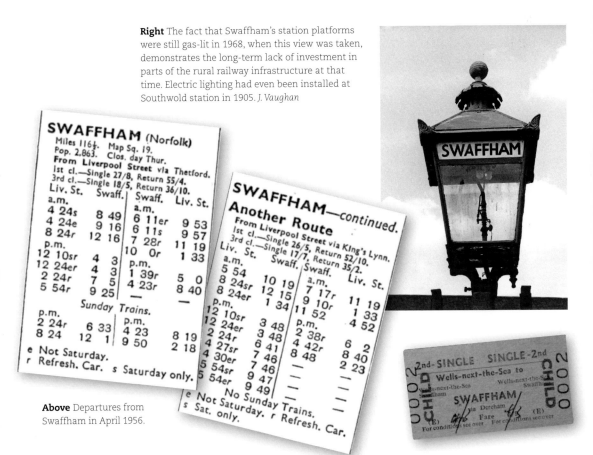

SWAFFHAM (Norfolk)
Miles 116¼. Map Sq. 19.
Pop. 2,863. Clos. day Thur.
From Liverpool Street via Thetford.
1st cl.—Single 27/8, Return 55/4.
3rd cl.—Single 18/5, Return 36/10.

Liv. St.	Swaff.	Swaff.	Liv. St.
a.m.		a.m.	
4 24s	8 49	6 11er	9 53
4 24e	9 16	6 11s	9 57
8 24r	12 16	7 28r	11 19
p.m.		10 0r	1 33
12 10sr	4 3	p.m.	
12 24er	4 3	1 39r	5 0
2 24r	7 5	4 23r	8 40
5 54r	9 25		

Sunday Trains.

p.m.		p.m.	
2 24r	6 33	4 23	
8 24	12 1	9 50	8 19
			2 18

e Not Saturday.
r Refresh. Car. s Saturday only.

Above Departures from Swaffham in April 1956.

SWAFFHAM—continued.
Another Route
From Liverpool Street via King's Lynn.
1st cl.—Single 26/5, Return 52/10.
3rd cl.—Single 17/7, Return 35/2.

Liv. St.	Swaff.	Swaff.	Liv. St.
a.m.		a.m.	
5 54	10 19	7 17r	11 19
8 24sr	12 15	9 10r	1 33
8 24er	1 34	11 52	4 52
12 10sr		p.m.	
12 24er	3 48	2 38r	6 2
2 24r	3 48	4 42r	8 40
4 27sr	6 41	8 48	2 23
4 30er	7 46		—
5 54sr	7 46		—
5 54er	9 47		—
	9 49		—

No Sunday Trains.

e Not Saturday. r Refresh. Car.
s Sat. only.

Below The 15.52 Norwich train leaves Swaffham past the ex-LNER signal box, which dated from 1926; the remaining signal arm has already been replaced to Danger. This view was taken on the last day of services, Saturday 7 September 1968. The abandoned water tower and most of the railway buildings still remained at that time. *G. Mortimer*

Above A Met-Cam DMU operating the 11.36 King's Lynn-Norwich service approaches Swaffham station on 3 September 1968, during the last week of the line. The attractive knapped-flint station building on the left survives in 2013. The train has just emerged from a long chalk cutting that had added to the construction costs of the railway.
G. Mortimer

Right On the last day that trains called at Narborough & Pentney, Saturday 7 September 1968, we see the 13.43 Norwich-King's Lynn service. Although the line itself was not recommended for closure in the Beeching Report, intermediate stations such as this were. The station building and platform canopy still survive in private ownership.
G. Mortimer

Facing page Glory days of the Hunstanton line: Class 'D15' 4-4-0 No 2507, still in LNER livery, heads the 5.50pm Hunstanton-Liverpool Street express at Wolferton in May 1949. The train crew prepare to hand over the token to the signalman for the single-line section north of Wolferton station; the line was then double-track south to King's Lynn. *Ian Allan Library*

Left Scenes of railway dereliction were to be found after closure of the Middleton Towers-Dereham section of line. Here East Winch station and signal box are seen looking towards King's Lynn in October 1976. The station buildings still survive, while the signal box was saved by the Mid-Norfolk Railway and relocated at Thuxton level crossing. *A. Muckley*

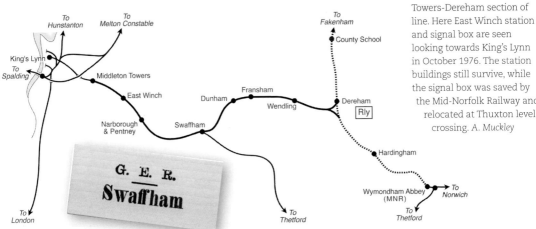

Right Although Swaffham had gas-lit platforms until the end, and some minor stations on the route remained with oil lamps, electricity was fully installed at Dereham by BR. The station, seen here in June 2012, remains in use as part of the preserved Mid-Norfolk Railway. *Author*

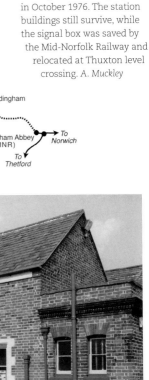

19

Hunstanton revisited

The 15¼-mile King's Lynn-Hunstanton line opened in October 1862. The resort flourished and the Sandringham Hotel, Norfolk's only railway-owned hotel, opened in 1876 next to Hunstanton station. The line also served Sandringham House and new station buildings were built at nearby Wolferton to impress Queen Victoria in the 1890s. The line became increasingly important for both its Royal Trains and holiday traffic to Hunstanton's sandy beaches.

In the 1920s there were numerous departures from Hunstanton to Liverpool Street, several with restaurant cars and including one service with Pullman coaches. Additional trains ran to and from King's Cross and other destinations. At peak times summer excursion trains resulted in the station being very busy. Even in the summer of 1964 there were through trains to and from London and other destinations.

Changes in holiday patterns led to the closing of the railway-owned hotel in 1950 and there was a general reduction in people using the train to reach British resorts from this time onwards. Initially BR made efforts to stimulate traffic and the line was not included in the closure proposals of the Beeching Report. The route also continued to be shown as a main line on some BR maps until the mid-1960s.

Right A 1910 advert for the GER's Sandringham Hotel, which adjoined Hunstanton station. Its popularity resulted in extensions in 1905 and 1920. The hotel was requisitioned during the Second World War, but as an alternative to refurbishment it was sold by BR to the local council in 1950. Bars and saloon lounges were kept open for a while, but the building was demolished in 1967. *Author's collection*

HUNSTANTON-ON-SEA.

Great Eastern Railway Company.

"SANDRINGHAM HOTEL"

ELECTRICALLY-LIGHTED THROUGHOUT.

BEAUTIFULLY SITUATED ON THE NORFOLK COAST.

FACING SEA.

SANDS UNRIVALLED FOR CHILDREN.

A Centre for Charming Country Excursions.

GOLF LINKS.   MOTORING.

Garage Electrically-lighted, with Private Boxes and Inspection Pits, &c. Tariff and other information from Resident Manager, or

H. C. AMENDT, Manager, G.E.R. Hotels,

Tel. No. 21 P.O. Hunstanton.   Liverpool St. Station.

A run-down of the line then began. Royal Trains ceased using Wolferton in 1966, through trains were withdrawn, all stations became unstaffed, ungated level crossings had to be passed at a crawling pace, and signalling was simplified. This in turn prevented excursion trains from being run on this 'basic railway', slowed trains and gave most stations a depressing run-down appearance. In 1967 the former railway hotel, which had been sold to the local council, was demolished. Winter receipts, as with many seaside resorts, were low and, after uproar, the route was closed in May 1969 – at the very beginning of the busy summer season. It was one of the more significant lines to close in East Anglia, and among the last to do so. Wolferton station is considered in more detail in *Lost Lines: Eastern*.

There was one branch off the Hunstanton route, from a junction at Heacham; this was the 18¼-mile Wells (name used until 1923) line, which opened in August 1866 'across the top of Norfolk'. Through

services were once provided to King's Lynn, but Wells never developed as such a popular resort as Hunstanton and passenger use was always limited. The link was an early closure to passengers in June 1952, when some of the few remaining gas-lit coaches in the country were still used on services. The section between Holkham and Wells-on-Sea (name used until 1957) was cut by floods in February 1953 and it was decided not to restore freight services over the damaged section, but the remaining Heacham-Burnham freight service survived until December 1964. All the station buildings on the branch remain in private ownership and a restored coach and former goods shed can be found at Burnham Market.

Right Departures from Hunstanton in April 1956.

Left Wolferton station was stylishly built to impress Queen Victoria, and here a decoratively crowned former gas lamp is seen in August 1994. Closure of the station, which served the royal estate at Sandringham, was not opposed by the royal household, who chose not to contribute to the upkeep of the station's royal waiting rooms. After closure in 1969, the station was sold and for a time was opened as a private museum. *Author*

HUNSTANTON

(Norfolk)

Miles 112¼. Map Sq. 14.

Pop. 3,414. Clos. day Thur.

REFRESHMENT ROOMS. Meals served during summer only.

From Liverpool Street.

1st cl.—Single. 26/5, Return 52/10.

3rd cl.—Single. 17/7, Return 35/2.

Liv. St. a.m.	Hunst. a.m.	Hunst. a.m.	Liv. St. a.m.
5 54	10 4	6 50er	9 53
8 24r	11 59	6 50s	9 57
p.m.	a.m.	7 46r	11 19
12 10sr	3 40	10 11r	1 33
12 24er	3 54	p.m.	
2 24r	5 59	12 36	
4 27sr	7 50	2 25r	4 52
4 30er	7 35	4 57r	6 2
5 54r	9 26	—	8 40
—			—

Sunday Trains.

a.m.	a.m.	a.m.	
8 24	12 0	9 0	12 37
p.m.		p.m.	
2 24r	6 5	2 38	6 33
5 54	9 27	4 40	7 58
—		6 7r	9 15
—	—	9 40	2 18

e Not Saturday.

r Refresh. Car. s Saturday only.

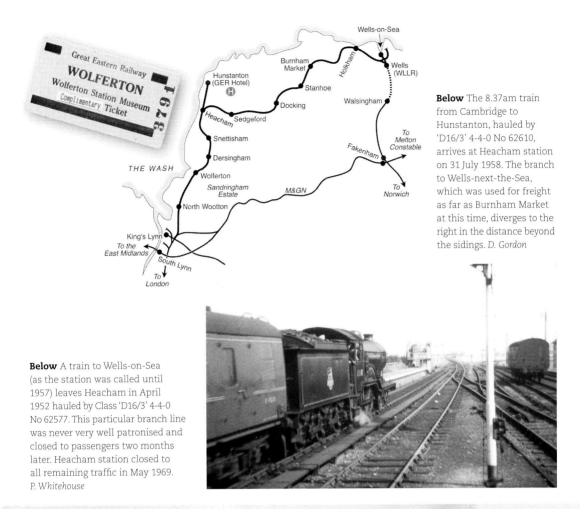

Great Eastern Railway
WOLFERTON
Wolferton Station Museum
Complimentary Ticket

Below The 8.37am train from Cambridge to Hunstanton, hauled by 'D16/3' 4-4-0 No 62610, arrives at Heacham station on 31 July 1958. The branch to Wells-next-the-Sea, which was used for freight as far as Burnham Market at this time, diverges to the right in the distance beyond the sidings. *D. Gordon*

Below A train to Wells-on-Sea (as the station was called until 1957) leaves Heacham in April 1952 hauled by Class 'D16/3' 4-4-0 No 62577. This particular branch line was never very well patronised and closed to passengers two months later. Heacham station closed to all remaining traffic in May 1969. *P. Whitehouse*

Left BTH Type 1 No D8216 receives the attention of some boys at Heacham station on 23 August 1960; it was one of the last of the class to be withdrawn, in 1971. The short train is the Heacham-Burnham Market daily goods. *B. Wykes*

Below The 2.04pm Hunstanton-King's Lynn DMU arrives at Snettisham station on 19 April 1969. The station once had camping coaches. Snettisham signal box survived after closure of the line and has since been re-erected at Hardingham station on the Mid-Norfolk Railway. *G. Mortimer*

Above Disused sidings are seen at Hunstanton in February 1969; the line closed the following May, just before the summer season began. There have been calls for reopening of this once busy line to help reduce summer road congestion, but this is looking ever more unlikely as the route is increasingly blocked by new development. *Author*

Above right Hunstanton station was well located beside the promenade. The pier, which can just be seen in the background beyond the deserted platforms, was damaged beyond repair in a storm in 1978. The desolation on a cold and wet February day in 1969 could not be more removed

from the peak summer activity. The station's refreshment room had long closed when this view was taken and all the remaining buildings seen here were demolished in 1971. *Author*

Below This BR Mark 1 1st Class coach is used as a 'camping coach' at Heacham station, as seen in June 2012. The coach and the well-preserved station house and platform buildings are now used as holiday accommodation. The track was removed in 1971, but almost all of the intermediate station buildings on the Hunstanton branch survive, in one form or another. *Author*

20

County School connections

Norfolk was once traversed by several GER secondary lines, but there was a gradual decline in the fortune of the railways in this rural area and cutbacks began, particularly after BR took over. Passenger numbers were generally limited, except to coastal resorts during peak summer holidays. Consequently agricultural freight was a lifeline for most branches, and sugar beet, potatoes, grain, malt, dairy and livestock, together with domestic coal, continued to be carried, in some cases long after passenger services ended.

Wells-next-the-Sea became the coastal terminus of a 21½-mile line that opened in December 1857, as an extension of the Wymondham-Dereham route. A branch to the harbour at Wells was completed two years later. The line ran through one of just two tunnels in Norfolk, at Barsham, but this was opened out in 1898.

Live shellfish were transported on passenger trains to London, but the 'dripping sacks' caused problems when DMUs were introduced. The Wells harbour branch once handled imported coal and exported agricultural produce, but a gradual silting of the harbour resulted in its decline and rail freight ceased in 1962. During the peak summer period passenger traffic was busy to the seaside town, while the religious centre of Walsingham also had some busy periods. However, in winter passenger traffic

Facing page On the night of 31 January/1 February 1953 the combination of a windstorm and an exceptionally high spring tide caused a massive tidal surge in the North Sea, resulting in serious flooding along the East Anglian coast. This aerial view, taken in early February, shows how the floods affected Wells-on-Sea station. The main line is centre left, the branch to Heacham upper left, and that to the harbour, which allowed the seawater to reach the station, in the left foreground. The flood damage between Wells and Burnham Market led to the premature closure of this section of line. *Ian Allan Library*

Below Wells-next-the-Sea (as the station was probably more aptly called from 1957) was a relatively large station for the size of the seaside port, and once had an adjoining engine shed. An animal feed mill was also located next to the station, and at times its smells mingled with those of the steam trains at the platforms. This view of the station was taken from the signal box on 13 June 1964. *Author*

was greatly reduced and all services to Wells ceased in October 1964.

At the southern end of the branch, Wymondham-North Elmham grain traffic ran until 1989. Since closure the Mid-Norfolk Railway, together with the 10¼-inch-gauge Wells & Walsingham Light Railway, has resulted in the return of trains to considerable sections of the Wymondham-Wells route.

Wroxham was reached in May 1882 by a 23¾-mile route from Broom Green on the Wells line. It was one of the last lines built by the GER, as a strategic link to prevent any rival Norwich-Aylsham railway being

constructed, and was used as part of an alternative and slower Norwich-Dereham service, via Wroxham and Aylsham South. In March 1884 the GER was persuaded to build a station south of Broom Green. This was called County School, because it served a nearby private school, and special trains were run at the beginning and end of term. The station also developed as the junction for the Wroxham line. The route to Wroxham was busy during the Second World War, serving RAF Coltishall in particular, but it closed to passengers in September 1952.

Freight remained, except between Reepham and Foulsham. At Lenwade, on the ex-M&GN line, there was a plant making prefabricated concrete products, and in September 1960 the Themelthorpe Curve was opened at the point where the ex-GER County School-Wroxham and ex-M&GN Melton Constable-Norwich City lines met. The curve provided a new shorter Lenwade-London link, via Aylsham South and Wroxham, rather than via Sheringham. The Lenwade traffic ended in 1981 and the line formally closed the following year. A final weed-killing train ran in October 1983, with track being removed in 1984-85. After closure, the 9-mile Aylsham South-Wroxham section was reopened as the 15-inch-gauge Bure Valley Railway in July 1990.

Wymondham was once also a junction for a 6¾-mile line south to Forncett on the main Norwich-London line. This link was opened in May 1881 and was built to relieve congestion in the Norwich area. At one time the link conveyed through London-Wells carriages. In September 1939 passenger services were suspended as a wartime economy measure, but were never resumed, while freight ceased in August 1951. However, a stub was retained to dismantle condemned rolling stock at Wymondham.

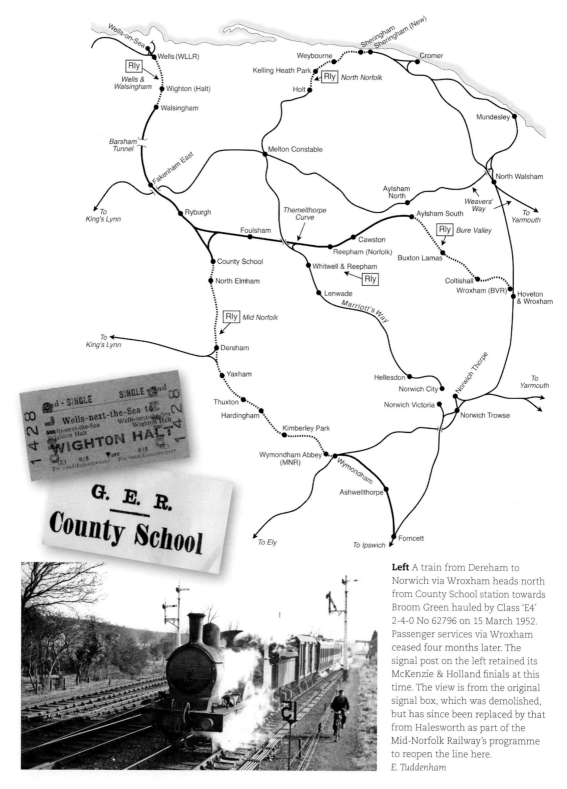

Left A train from Dereham to Norwich via Wroxham heads north from County School station towards Broom Green hauled by Class 'E4' 2-4-0 No 62796 on 15 March 1952. Passenger services via Wroxham ceased four months later. The signal post on the left retained its McKenzie & Holland finials at this time. The view is from the original signal box, which was demolished, but has since been replaced by that from Halesworth as part of the Mid-Norfolk Railway's programme to reopen the line here.
E. Tuddenham

4109

SPECIAL CHEAP DAY TICKETS
ANY DAY ANY TRAIN

AVAILABLE OUTWARD AND RETURN ON DAY OF ISSUE FROM

DEREHAM
FAKENHAM

TO

	Return fares second class	
	Dereham	Fakenham
	s. d.	s. d.
County School	2 0	2 0
Dereham		3 0
Dunham	2 4	5 3
East Winch	5 3	8 0
Fakenham (East)	3 0	
Fransham	2 0	4 9
Hardingham	1 8	4 2
Hethersett	3 6	5 9
Hunstanton	9 9	
Kimberley Park	2 0	4 6
King's Lynn	6 0*	9 0
Lowestoft (Central)	10 6	
Middleton Towers	5 6	8 3
Narborough and Pentney	4 2	7 3
North Elmham	1 8	2 3
Norwich (Thorpe)	4 0*	6 3
Ryburgh	2 6	1 2
Swaffham	3 0	6 0
Thuxton	1 4	3 9
Walsingham	4 2	1 6
Wells-next-the-Sea	5 3	2 8
Wendling	1 6	4 6
Wighton Halt	4 9	2 0
Wymondham	2 9	5 2
Yarmouth (Vauxhall)	8 6	10 9
Yaxham	9	3 4

*—Return halves of Special Cheap Day Tickets Dereham to King's Lynn and Norwich (Thorpe) and vice versa are alternatively available between those points by the Eastern Counties Omnibus Company's road services

First class tickets are also issued at approximately 50 per cent over the above fares where first class accommodation is available

Children under three years of age, free; three years and under fourteen, approximately half-fares

Passengers may alight at a station short of destination upon surrender of the ticket, and commence the return journey from an intermediate station

Tickets can be obtained IN ADVANCE

Further information will be supplied on application to stations, offices, travel agents appointed by British Railways or to:
Traffic Manager, Norwich (Thorpe) (Tel: Norwich 20371)

London, February 1963

GREAT EASTERN

THIS SUPERSEDES HANDBILL 4106

Published by British Railways (Eastern Region)   Printed in Great Britain   Modern Press (Norwich) Ltd

Above A map of County School station and Broom Green, where the line diverged eastwards towards Wroxham, in 1949. *Crown Copyright*

Left A BR handbill from 1963.

Right This is the view looking north from County School station platform towards Broom Green and the present signal box in June 2012. This marks the current end of the track, which stretches all the way south to Wymondham. The station at County School has been restored to its original condition and provides a tea room. *Author*

21

M&GN mementos

The closure of most of the ex-M&GN in February 1959 was a bitter foretaste of what was to come in East Anglia, with the Beeching cuts of the following decade. Once the main ex-M&GN closure had taken place a number of short sections remained, mainly to honour existing freight contracts. This residue of lines soon also closed and it might be thought that remnants of the railway would gradually disappear over the many decades since the last trains ran.

Yet remains are surprisingly numerous, and along the closed lines a remarkable amount can still be found. Some significant bridges are extant, in particular the swing bridge at the aptly named Sutton Bridge and the huge cast-iron supports of the West Lynn Bridge, together with unique 'A'-framed bridges on the Norwich City line. In addition several other interesting bridges are still to be found and are often of individual designs; these sometimes reflect the different constituent railways that formed the M&GN, or later additions by the LNER.

Stations have also survived, including Sheringham and Weybourne, which continue under the auspices of the North Norfolk Railway, while Stalham station buildings were re-erected at Holt. Whitwell station has also seen the return of trains. Cromer Beach station buildings still remain, but are no longer directly used by the railway. Elsewhere the

Facing page The sturdy cast-iron columns of West Lynn Bridge, or Clenchwarton Bridge as it was also known, still survived when this view was taken in November 2009. A 10mph speed limit was eventually imposed on the bridge and the need to renew the single-track deck of the 490-foot (150-metre) bridge, which dated from 1864, was cited as one of the main reasons for the closure of the entire M&GN network. The deck was removed in October 1959. *Author*

Right A number of distinctive ex-M&GN river bridges remain, as shown by this view of the navigable River Nene from the control tower of Sutton Bridge, also known as Cross Keys Bridge. Signal levers and equipment for the swing bridge were provided by Sir W. C. Armstrong Whitworth & Co of Newcastle in 1897 and remained in use when this view was taken in August 1994, although no longer connected to the signal boxes on each side of the now all-road bridge. However, even at this time an ex-LNER lamp still provided a warning for river shipping. *Author*

stations at Attlebridge, Bluestone, Grimston Road, Hillington, Hindolvestone, Lenwade and Raynham Park are all used as private residences. Felmingham, Gedney and Holbeach were all derelict in 2012. Corpusty & Saxthorpe station is used by the local sports club. Part of the platforms at Fakenham West and Honing survive, while smaller platform remains at Norwich City and Hellesdon are also to be found.

A number of signal boxes have survived, with Cromer Beach, Sheringham East and Weybourne box, relocated from Holt, all seeing trains pass by. Honing box has also been resited on a private railway near Wroxham. Massingham, Langor Bridge and Hindolvestone signal boxes all endure on disused sections of the M&GN.

Even the huge iron water tower at Melton Constable survives, together with some general railway buildings at this once important M&GN

railway town. Elsewhere throughout the former network, from huge goods sheds to small platelayer huts, many remains are still to be found. Thousands of items of railwayana also survive in museums and private collections.

The Aylsham-Norwich 'Marriott's Way' uses the ex-M&GN trackbed for 26 miles; the walk is named after the M&GN's charismatic Engineer, Locomotive Superintendent and Traffic Manager, who was involved with the railway for many years. The 'Weavers' Way' also follows several miles of ex-M&GN line near North Walsham. Other sections are in use as footpaths, farm tracks and roads.

Today only the Cromer-Holt section is still used by trains, with the Sheringham-Holt line being operated by the North Norfolk Railway. Whitwell station is also preserved as a railway centre. Yet it is clear that the M&GN remains hugely popular and a message written on one of the last trains in 1959 – 'The M&GN will never die' – proved to have remarkable prophecy.

Left This ornate cast-iron and steel road overbridge, south of Honing station, dates from 1881 and was photographed in November 2012. The elegant structure, with panels decorated with trefoils, included slender lattice legs. The bridge is now over the 'Weavers' Way', a long-distance footpath that uses much of the ex-M&GN Aylsham-Stalham trackbed. The differing designs of bridges was due in part to the earlier constituent railways that were amalgamated into the M&GN. *Author*

Below The Norwich City-Melton Constable line passed over the River Wensum just north of Lenwade station. Bridge No 261, dating from 1882, is seen here in April 2009. The bridge foundations were constructed for a possible doubling of the single line. The bridge now carries the 'Marriott's Way' long-distance footpath, named after the M&GN's resourceful and long-serving Engineer, Locomotive Superintendent and Traffic Manager. *Author*

Right Bridge No 249, an 'A'-framed bridge over the River Wensum at Hellesdon, on a well-used section of the 'Marriott's Way' near Norwich, is seen in October 2012. The 'A' frame provided additional strength to the girder bridge, which was completed by 1882. This is one of two surviving 'A'-framed bridges on the ex-M&GN. *Author*

Below Construction of Jellicoe Road bridge at Newtown, north of Yarmouth Beach station, was started by the LNER in 1936, but was not completed until 1948. Although crossing a single line, provision was made for possible eventual doubling of the route, such were the expectations for rail holiday traffic growth prior to the Second World War. The mainly concrete bridge, with parapets of brick and local flint, is seen here in November 2012. *Author*

Below Barnard Avenue bridge, also north of Yarmouth Beach station, was made from reinforced concrete. Again the bridge was designed for double track and was part of a pre-Second World War LNER project to improve the operation of the railway north of Yarmouth Beach and at Caister. An elegant art deco part of the bridge parapet is seen here in November 2012. *Author*

Facing page Class 'J15' 0-6-0 No 65422 leaves the East harbour freight branch at Wisbech with the daily freight to March in April 1953. The branch skirted round the town to serve industrial areas and the east side harbour areas on the River Nene, which is navigable to the sea. The train is seen passing over the abandoned Wisbech & Outwell Canal. *P. Lynch*

Left This bridge on the NSJ, which was a joint operation by the M&GN and GER, was built in blue engineering bricks and dates from 1906. The road bridge was skilfully positioned to afford pedestrian access to the island platform of Trimingham station, as well as providing a station store under the footbridge section, seen here jutting out from the main road bridge in July 2008. The line was an early casualty, closing in April 1953. *Author*

Right Expanding development and the new Norwich ring road necessitated the construction of two new bridges over the line north of Norwich City station. The bridges were mostly built of concrete blocks and opened in 1923. The existing telephone wires were directed under the new bridges and some metal supports for porcelain insulators still survive, as can be seen in this view taken in October 2012. *Author*

22

Withdrawals from Wisbech

Wisbech, an important market town and inland seaport on the navigable River Nene, was once well connected by railways. The first railway to the town was the 7¾-mile line from March, opening in 1847. In February 1848 the line was extended 9¾ miles to Watlington, later renamed Magdalen Road, and services ran on to King's Lynn. The east harbour branch was built at Wisbech in 1863 and the first station developed as a goods yard known as South Bank.

Such was the importance of the town that another line on the west side of the River Nene was opened in August 1866, later to become part of the M&GN. A harbour branch was constructed to the western banks of the River Nene, but the harbour lines on either side of the river were never connected, due to concerns about another bridge crossing the navigable river. However, together the railways helped develop Wisbech's importance as a port for agricultural produce, timber, coal and other merchandise.

Prior to the Second World War some 50-70 wagons a day, loaded with freight including Baltic timber, coal, and Scotch seed potatoes, would use the East harbour branch. Wagons of oranges and lemons would also be delivered on a regular basis to the private sidings of a nearby marmalade factory. The branch became progressively less well used after the war, but survived until 1966.

At the turn of the 20th century roads in the area were in a generally poor condition, but it was a very fertile agricultural district and a Wisbech-Upwell

branch line was planned by the GER. Being unable to raise sufficient funds for a railway, a tramway was proposed instead under the 1870 Tramways Act. It opened from Wisbech East station to Outwell Basin in August 1883 and reached Upwell in September 1884. Proposals for an extension to Welney and through the streets of Wisbech to the main market were abandoned, but the tramway acted as an important freight feeder to the main-line station.

The roadside tramway had an original speed restriction of 8mph, but this was later raised to 12mph and passenger trains on the tramway were 'speeded up' from 60 to 39 minutes for the 6-mile journey. Yet the tramway could still not compete with buses and the LNER withdrew passenger services in December 1927, the first major closure in the area. Freight traffic remained buoyant in this fertile area, particularly during the fruit and potato seasons, when wagons and vans were sometimes unable to meet demand.

In 1952 the line became the first all-diesel-operated route in the country and the steam shed was rebuilt to accommodate the new diesel tram engines. At the same time lorries were taking away more and

Above The glass portico on the exterior of Wisbech East station is seen in 1953. The ex-GER station was renamed East after the railways were nationalised in 1948, to distinguish it from the ex-M&GN station in the town, which became the North station. *Ian Allan Library*

more of the line's freight traffic. Economies were made and individual goods depots on the tramway such as Boyce's Bridge depot and Outwell Village station were closed. Yet in the mass of closures of the 1960s this last roadside tramway in Britain did not finally succumb until May 1966. Remarkably, one of the passenger tramcars, No 7 dating from 1884, still survives.

Wisbech North station had closed to passengers in February 1959, as part of the extensive closure of the ex-M&GN network. However, the West harbour branch was reached from a new spur at Murrow on the ex-GN&GE line. Freight ran on this section until January 1965 and to Wisbech North station until October of that year.

At one time through coaches of 'The Fenman' express were routed via Wisbech East and the station was busy with passengers. There were through services to and from many main centres and the line was not considered for closure in the Beeching Report. Sadly the remaining line closed to passengers in September 1968, and today nothing remains of either station in the town.

The March-Wisbech East goods yard line survived in freight use until 2000 and, although officially closed in 2002, the remaining single line from March to the outskirts of Wisbech is still extant. There have been proposals put forward for the reuse of this line as part of the national rail network, as Wisbech's population is now more than 20,000, while the Bramley Line Heritage Railway Trust has also expressed interest in reopening the line as a heritage route.

Below Class 'J70' 0-6-0T tram engine No 68222, dating from 1914, is seen at Wisbech East station on the Wisbech & Upwell Tramway in June 1952. This was shortly before dieselisation of the route, although this steam tram was retained for emergency purposes until March 1953. The engine's spark arrestor, skirts enclosing the motion and cow-catchers for roadside working are all to be noted. *P. Ransome-Wallis*

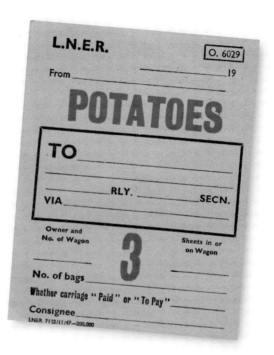

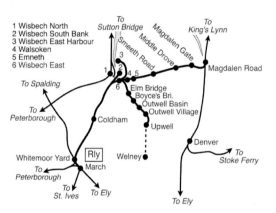

1 Wisbech North
2 Wisbech South Bank
3 Wisbech East Harbour
4 Walsoken
5 Emneth
6 Wisbech East

To Sutton Bridge
To King's Lynn
Magdalen Gate
Middle Drove
Smeeth Road
Magdalen Road
To Spalding
Elm Bridge
Boyce's Bri.
Outwell Basin
Outwell Village
To Peterborough
Coldham
Upwell
Denver
Whitemoor Yard
Rly
Welney
To Stoke Ferry
To Peterborough
March
To St. Ives
To Ely
To Ely

Above A very lengthy freight train is seen near the village of Outwell on the Wisbech & Upwell Tramway on 24 August 1950, hauled by Class 'J70' 0-6-0T tram engine No 68217, dating from 1903 and withdrawn in 1953. During the height of the fruit season freight was heavy, and up to 100 vans could be seen in sidings at Upwell. *H. C. Casserley*

Below All services on the remaining March-Wisbech branch had ceased by 2000 and the end of the track at Wisbech is seen here in June 2012. At Wisbech the remaining track is considerably overgrown, and where the line crosses the A47 it has been removed, making reopening ever more difficult. At the March end of the rusting line the track was relatively clear of vegetation in 2013 and there remains strong support for reopening. *Author*

WISBECH (Cambs)
Miles 93¾. Map Sq. 18.
Pop. 17,430. Clos. day Wed.
EAST STATION.
From Liverpool Street via March.
1st cl.—Single 22/2, Return 44/4.
3rd cl.—Single 14/9, Return 29/6.

Liv. St.	Wisb.	Wisb.	Liv. St.
a.m.		a.m.	
5 54	9 43	7 30er	9 53
8 24r	11 36	7 30s	9 57
p.m.		8 37r	11 19
12 10sr	3 17	11 25p	2 36
12 24er	3 17	p.m.	
2 24r	5 47	2 45r	6 2
4 27sr	7 16	5 5r	8 40
4 30er	7 3	11 1e	2 23
7 24dr	10 8	—	—
8 50s	11 49	—	—
10 24e	2 59	—	—

Sunday Trains.

a.m.		a.m.	
8 24	11 31	9 35	12 37
p.m.		p.m.	
2 24r	6 3	3 35	6 33
8 24	11 9	6 55r	9 15

d Wed. only.   e Not Sat.
p Refresh. Car on Saturday.
r Refresh. Car. s Saturday only.

Another Route
NORTH STATION.
From King's Cross via Peterborough.
1st cl.—Single 22/11. Return 45/10.
3rd cl.—Single 15/3, Return 30/6.

Kg's X	Wisb.	Wisb.	Kg's X
a.m.		a.m.	
3 50	7 21	7 46r	10 35
8 20r	11 17	10 23er	1 3
10 20r	1 32	10 23sr	1 10
p.m.		p.m.	
2 0r	4 25	12 32q	4 12
4 0r	6 38	1 32mr	3 50
6 18r	8 59	1 32qr	4 48
—	—	2 24sr	4 48
—	—	4 12sr	7 34
—	—	4 25f	7 25
—	—	4 25er	7 34
—	—	6 34r	9 36

No Sunday Trains.
e Not Saturday. f Friday only.
m Monday, Friday & Saturday.
q Tuesday, Wednesday & Thurs.
r Refresh. Car. s Saturday only.

Above Departures from Wisbech in April 1956.

Above Drewry shunter No D2201, fitted with skirts and cow-catchers for tramway working, stands at Wisbech with the final train to Upwell on Friday 20 May 1966, comprising just a brake van in order to bring back remaining rolling stock to Wisbech. Many wide verges on the Wisbech-Upwell road still provide evidence of the tramway's former route. *L. Sandler*

Left No D2201 passes Outwell Church with three open wagons and a brake van from Upwell to Wisbech, the final working on the tramway on 20 May 1966. The Wisbech Canal, abandoned for commercial traffic in 1926 but surviving at this point for pleasure craft, can be seen to the left of the tramway. Tramway Road at this location still provides a reminder of the line. *L. Sandler*

23

Whitemoor Marshalling Yard

As freight traffic between London and East Anglia and the North of England continued to increase, together with mounting sugar beet traffic, a number of goods yards in East Anglia became congested and there were mounting delays to the vast flows of freight. The railway strike of 1927 led to the entire Coldham-March line being packed with coal trucks, and it became evident that something had to be done. The flat fenland adjoining the railway junctions at March proved an ideal site for a marshalling yard, and the first Whitemoor yard was opened in March 1929, by the LNER. It had more than 40 sidings with a total length of about 30 miles.

The hump yard was equipped with German Fröhlich hydraulic retarders, the first use of such wagon brakes in this country. The yard had a capacity for about 4,000 wagons. When a freight train arrived at the reception sidings the engine was detached, wagons were uncoupled and a 'cut card' made out; the 'cuts' were the number of wagons in the train that needed to be uncoupled and sent to various sidings. This information was dispatched to the control tower by a pneumatic tube. The control tower then set the electric points and the wagons, if necessary, were slowed to a suitable speed by the retarders; this largely depended on the number of wagons already in the chosen siding, as the wagons were intended

Facing page This view of Whitemoor marshalling yard control tower was taken in June 1929, the year the yard opened. The LNER control tower was also variously called the control centre, control box or hump cabin and had a German influence in its design. The building's overview of the yard and control of points and retarders enabled up to 70 wagons to be marshalled in 7 minutes. *Ian Allan Library*

to stop short of or hit the existing wagons very slowly. Over time the operators 'sensed' the wagon speeds through experience, but a loudspeaker system provided instructions from the control tower to key staff in the yard to enable individual wagon brakes to be applied if necessary.

The first three-position semaphore signals in Britain were provided on the approach to the hump. If the arm was at 45% from horizontal with an orange light displayed, the driver had to proceed at a normal shunting speed, but if it was at 90%, i.e. vertical, and a green light was displayed the driver could proceed towards the hump at a faster speed.

In February 1931 the down yard was added, comprising almost 40 sidings with a length of about 30 miles. Further extensions were made, and by the end of the 1930s Whitemoor became the second largest marshalling yard in Europe. At the start of the Second World War up to 8,000 wagons could be sorted each day, and the total site covered some 250 acres (101 hectares). The importance of the yard was highlighted during the war when decoy lights were set up in fields 4 miles away and turned on during the 'blackout' to confuse enemy bombers, while the real yard was in darkness. As it happened Germany never targeted the yard.

In June 1944 a Whitemoor-Ipswich ammunition train left the yard with 51 wagons containing 400 tons of bombs. The engine driver was Ben Gimbert and the fireman Jim Nightall. On approaching Soham the driver noticed flames from one of the wagons. The fireman detached the burning wagon from the rest of the train, but as they started to pull it away it exploded, killing the fireman and severely injuring the driver, but much reducing the impact had the entire train exploded. Both men were awarded the George Cross.

Adjoining Whitemoor marshalling yard was March engine shed (31B); this had more than 200 locomotives allocated in 1947, with heavy freight engines dominating, to haul trains to and from the yard. By 1959 the allocation had reduced to 131 locomotives, and the steam shed closed in 1963 when diesel traction took over.

In the 1960s BR provided some named freight trains to and from the yard, such as the 'Lea Valley

Right This general view of Whitemoor marshalling yard from the control tower was taken on 15 May 1930. When the down yard was added the following year the original yard and control tower became the up yard and Whitemoor became the largest marshalling yard in Britain. This somewhat bleak, flat and open fenland was an ideal location for such a yard, but the scale of the sidings still required substantial earthworks to be carried out. *Ian Allan Library*

Enterprise' and the 'East Essex Enterprise', but the mass scrapping of unfitted freight wagons and loss of rail freight generally spelled the end for the yard. In 1974 the down yard closed as a hump, while the up hump continued until 1980. In 1982 the March-Spalding section of the ex-GN&GE closed, and by 1984 most sidings in the down yard had been removed. The up sidings were now the only part of the yard to be used, but were gradually phased out as remaining freight traffic was concentrated at Peterborough. Official closure came in 1990, and the last sidings became derelict during the following decade.

After closure the remaining track was gradually pulled up and much of the area remained as a wasteland. Some new civil engineers' sidings were opened in 2004, then in July 2011 Britain's biggest rail recycling depot, with its own associated new sidings, was opened on part of the original yard and steam shed.

Below Whitemoor, with the hump leading towards the control tower and the fan of sidings beyond, is seen again in May 1930. Some wagons containing fragile products carried notices 'not to be hump shunted' and had to be taken directly into the yard by locomotives avoiding the hump. 'Not to be hump shunted' notices could still be seen on some rolling stock in 2013. *Ian Allan Library*

Above One of the four retarders at Whitemoor made by the German firm of Fröhlich is seen in close-up on 15 May 1930. They were essentially a hydraulic wagon brake that gripped the side of the wheel flanges, slowing wagons down sufficiently to separate them and to prevent any heavy impact when they hit standing wagons in the various sidings. The first use of this type of retarder in Britain was at Whitemoor, but they could cause damage to wagon frames and Westinghouse equipment was used in the later down yard. *Ian Allan Library*

Right Wagons pass over the hump into the down yard at Whitemoor. The wagons in the centre of the view have just commenced their run down a short gradient of 1 in 18 under gravity, while the wagon on the right is the end wagon of a train moving slowly towards the hump. The control tower can be seen on the left in this view from 23 February 1947. *N. Robinson*

Below Radio installations at Whitemoor are seen inside the control tower on 17 March 1949, soon after they were first introduced. The radio control provided direct contact with diesel shunting engines in the yard, which were also equipped with speedometers. At the time this was such an innovation that the project featured in Pathé News. *BR*

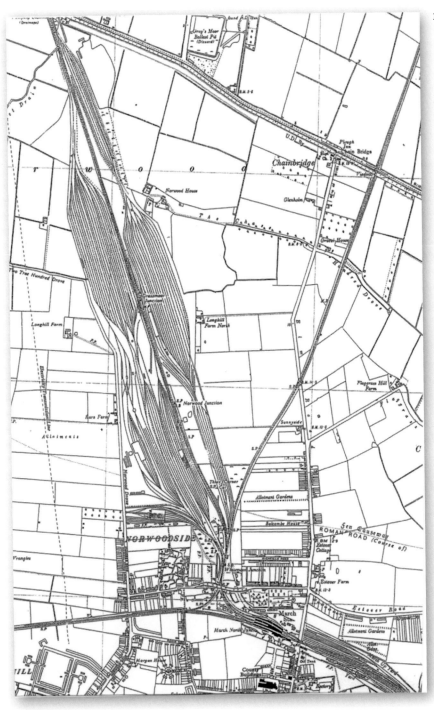

Left A map of Whitemoor marshalling yard in 1941. The closed March-Spalding line runs between the main up and down hump yards, while the closed March-Wisbech line is on the right. Norwood Yard and March locomotive depot are to the south of the two main hump yards. *Crown Copyright*

Facing page top This was the view of the control tower and yard from the hump at Whitemoor in 1949, as coal trucks descend into the sidings. Note the change in the floodlighting columns, which were designed to be less visible from the air than the pre-war lighting seen in earlier views. Later taller gantry lights were installed before closure. *BR*

Facing page bottom A number of the LNER concrete cable carriers seen in earlier views were among the few remains of the original freight yard to survive and are glimpsed here in April 2012. Parts of the yard area have been redeveloped, while part has also been reused by Network Rail. *Author*

24

Preserving the past

A number of heritage railways and museums have undertaken remarkable work in saving and restoring sections of line, locomotives, rolling stock and railwayana from East Anglian railways. All provide a real opportunity to return to the past world of lost lines and offer railway journeys of various lengths. Furthermore, some items of railway equipment, stock and locomotives, seen in earlier photographs in this book, can be found preserved at the various railway centres.

Heritage lines in Essex include the 6¼-mile Epping Ongar Railway and the 1-mile Colne Valley Railway, at Castle Hedingham. Other railway centres are established at the Mangapps Farm Railway Museum, at Burnham-on-Crouch, and the East Anglian Railway Museum, at Chappel & Wakes Colne station, on the Sudbury branch, both featuring vast collections of railwayana and stock. The Audley End Miniature Railway also has 1½ miles of line.

In Suffolk the Mid-Suffolk Light Railway centre is located at Wetheringsett, with the Dr Ian C. Allan Museum. The East Anglia Transport Museum, at Carlton Colville, near Lowestoft, has a narrow-gauge line and an ex-Southwold Railway luggage van. The Southwold Railway Trust is dedicated to preserving the memory of this narrow-gauge railway and is aiming to reopen a section of line. The Long Shop Museum, at the former Garrett's works at Leiston, runs *Sirapite*,

Facing page The Epping Ongar Railway provides a heritage line at the Essex end of an ex-GER branch line. At one time the branch became part of London Underground's Central Line, before services were suspended in 1994. A Class 37 diesel-electric restored as No D6729 in BR green livery is seen at North Weald in August 2012, after the reopening of the line earlier that year. *A. Axcell*

Below right The East Anglian Railway Museum is located at Chappel & Wakes Colne station on the Sudbury branch. This restored cast-iron open-air urinal, formerly on the platform at Cockfield station and seen in an earlier photograph in this book, is seen again in the summer of 2012. The Macfarlane's patented device, as with numerous other cast-iron urinals, was made at Saracen Foundry in Glasgow, and is just one of many exhibits at the museum. *Author*

delightful, together with most of today's rail staff – they all deserve a vote of thanks.

None of these preserved lines, museums or, for that matter, the existing East Anglian branch lines of the national rail network are entirely safe without our support and patronage. Someone once said that as you grow older the only things that you regret are those things that you did not do, so go and enjoy the many railway delights of East Anglia – you will not regret it.

a cross between a locomotive and a traction engine, and has plans to reopen the railway that ran between the Town Works and the main-line station.

The great loss of lines in Norfolk has, if nothing else, been of some benefit to the preservation movement. The 5-mile North Norfolk Railway operates the Sheringham-Holt section of the ex-M&GN, and among its many items from East Anglian railways is a coach from the Wisbech & Upwell Tramway. Whitwell is another ex-M&GN preserved railway station with stock and public access.

The Mid-Norfolk Railway operates over a substantial part of the 17½-mile ex-GER line between Wymondham, Dereham and County School, with plans to possibly eventually reach Fakenham. Elsewhere the 9-mile Aylsham-Wroxham Bure Valley Railway and the 4-mile Wells & Walsingham Light Railway are narrow-gauge lines that use former standard gauge ex-GER branch trackbeds. Short lines are also to be found at Wells Harbour, Yaxham, Barton House and at other locations throughout East Anglia.

One of the early railway centres in East Anglia was the Bressingham Steam Experience, near Diss, where 2½ miles of narrow gauge line are complemented by a standard-gauge line and stock. It was created by Alan Bloom, who once signed a neighbour's book and covered it with engine oil – she was far from pleased!

Alan Bloom was one of an often unsung band of railway enthusiasts who work hard and dig deep into their pockets to help preserve key items of railway heritage. Equally there were those professional railwaymen that made my travels as a schoolboy so

Right In the preserved booking office at Chappel & Wakes Colne, photographed in April 2013, is the wooden luggage label storage chest used to house almost 100 different luggage labels. The individual pigeonhole doors could be slid open and closed. In some cases, in the interests of efficiency by the staff, the tiny doors disappeared altogether. *Author*

Below right The Colne Valley Railway's reconstructed station at Castle Hedingham is seen in June 2012. The station building, with its distinctive brickwork, was dismantled from Sible & Castle Hedingham and re-erected beside the original CVR trackbed at the preserved railway in 1976. The railway aims to recreate as much as possible of the original CVR. *Author*

Below The Mangapps Farm Railway Museum at Burnham-on-Crouch has the ex-MSL timber-framed and corrugated-iron-clad waiting room from Laxfield station, seen here in August 2012. Horham station from the MSL is also preserved on the site. The museum has a vast collection of railwayana collected from throughout East Anglia. *Author*

Above The Mid-Suffolk Light Railway is located on the site of Brockford & Wetheringsett station's original cattle dock. The station building was restored from original buildings on the line and is seen here in August 1994. The Dr Ian C. Allan Museum on the site provides a history of 'The Middy'. Note the distinctive shape of the original MSL level crossing gate warning panel. *Author*

Above Many other smaller items from the M&GN remain. The use of reinforced concrete was widely developed by William Marriott, and here a preserved concrete milepost is seen. The M&GN initials were only cast on the full mileposts. Such was their quality of the concrete products made at Melton Constable that those not deliberately destroyed still survive in excellent condition. *Author*

Left The East Anglian Transport Museum at Carlton Colville near Lowestoft, seen here in September 1999, contains the only remaining item of Southwold Railway rolling stock, one of the railway's two luggage vans. The van body had been located on the platform at Southwold station for many years and has since been rewheeled. Smaller items from the narrow-gauge line can also be found at the Southwold Museum. The level crossing cabin is from the NSJ line at Lowestoft and is now on the Mid-Norfolk Railway. *Author*

Above The North Norfolk Railway, 'The Poppy Line', operates over the Sheringham-Holt section of the M&GN. This view at Sheringham was taken in 1970, with permission, and shows the only surviving Class 'J15' 0-6-0, No 65462. The line provides marvellous views over this part of the Norfolk coast and a connection is provided to the main-line network at Sheringham. *Author*

Above The Whitwell & Reepham Railway features a faithful reproduction M&GN platform oil lamp, seen here at Whitwell station in April 2009. The restored station is characteristic of many on the M&GN and oil-lit platforms survived at smaller stations until closure of most of the line to passenger traffic in 1959. *Author*

The Wells & Walsingham Railway opened in 1982 and is the longest 10¼-inch-gauge line in the world, using the ex-GER Wells-Walsingham trackbed. A train from Walsingham is seen arriving at Wells narrow-gauge station in June 2012. The signal box was rescued from Swainsthorpe, but the name board is from the original Wells box. *Author*

The Mid-Norfolk Railway connects the market towns of
Wymondham and Dereham and has ambitions to eventually
run the entire length of the former GER line between
Wymondham and Fakenham. A diesel shunter and Class 20
'Chopper' No D8069 are seen at County School in September
1994. After closure by BR in 1964, this site temporarily lost
its trains again in 1999, but it remains a visitor centre and
will be reconnected to the Mid-Norfolk Railway. *Author*

Left This is the Bure Valley Railway's
terminus at Aylsham in September
1994. Opened in 1990, 15-inch-gauge
trains use the trackbed of the ex-GER
standard-gauge Aylsham South-
Wroxham line. A footbridge at Wroxham
connects the railway to the main line.
Author

Left The Bressingham Steam Experience is a fitting name, as demonstrated by this photo taken from the cab of BR Standard Class 7 4-6-2 No 70013 *Oliver Cromwell* in September 1969, when footplate rides were being given. In 2008 the locomotive was returned to main-line working, some 40 years after it worked the last BR steam service. *Author*

Below In addition to preserved railways a number of special trains are run on the national network. No 70013 *Oliver Cromwell* is seen again, this time passing Woodbridge station in May 2009 on one such special (Oliver Cromwell's severed head was at one time stored at Woodbridge). Today the station, once proposed for closure by Dr Beeching, has seen passenger numbers double in less than a decade. *Author*

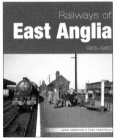
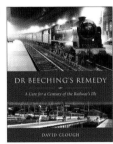
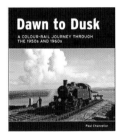
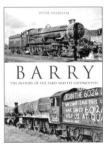

A nostalgic and memorable 'then and now' portrait of lost lines
in one of the most scenic parts of the country

❂

A follow-up and companion volume to the author's first successful volume,
Lost Lines: Eastern and detailing over 30 routes not prviously covered

❂

Includes a fascinating selection of historic and present day
photographs, maps and railway ephemera

www.ianallanpublishing.com

ISBN 978-0-7110-3748-9

9 780711 037489

Printed in England

£18.00